North Country Trail

Ice Age Trail

New England Trail

Potomac Heritage Trail

Appalachian Trail

Natchez Trace Trail

Florida Trail

N

0   200 miles   400 miles

AMERICA'S GREAT
HIKING TRAILS

KAREN BERGER

PHOTOGRAPHY BY
BART SMITH

FOREWORD BY
BILL McKIBBEN

RIZZOLI
NEW YORK

New York · Paris · London · Milan

CONTENTS

FOREWORD

I live about four hiking miles from the Long Trail, America's oldest long-distance hiking path. If I walk out the door and down an abandoned Forest Service road and then up a foot-trail, I find myself on the spine of the Green Mountains, and at a signpost pointing north to Canada and south to the Massachusetts border. More, I find myself on a corridor where dozens of people a day (hundreds on a hot summer day) wander by. Most are day trippers, but a grizzled and hardy few are going all the way. And it's to those I'm most drawn.

That's because they've learned the secret of long-distance hikes, which is that in a connected, digital, busy world, there's still a way to actually leave the buzz behind for a while. The mere existence of one of these lines on a map has given them permission to dream and then to act—to head off with relative safety into the woods and just keep going. And going. And going. And when you do the same? After a few days, the chatter of the world starts to drop away—your world becomes this narrow corridor, and the distance to the next lean-to, and the ache in your back. If you're really lucky, the nonstop CNN of your brain (the hopes, the fears, the plans, the to-do lists) starts to drop away and you can actually be where you are. A long hiking trail is a kind of meditation, done not in robes but in Gore-Tex.

Over the years I've had the great fortune to hike portions of many of these trails—the Appalachian Trail over the Bigelows of Maine, or through the Sterling Forest on the New York-New Jersey border (rattlesnakes and bears an hour from Times Square!). I've wandered those sections of the Pacific Crest Trail through the unbearably beautiful Tuolumne granite. And I've known some of the people who pioneered these paths: I think of the day in Idaho's Salmon-Challis National Forest when I met Walkin' Jim Stoltz, who walked every year from Mexico to Canada, scouting out new possible trails. (By the time I got to know him, he'd stopped even taking maps. He was just following game paths through the canyons.) The many people we hikers owe a debt for these trails (above all Benton MacKaye, the father of the Appalachian Trail) thought on a large scale. They saw connections. They sensed the possibility of both community and distance. Thank heaven (and John Muir) for their vision.

And thanks for the vision they've inspired in all of us who get to follow in their literal footsteps. Here in Vermont, in the 1930s when the Long Trail was already some decades old, the federal government offered to build a highway, à la the Blue Ridge Parkway, along the spine of the Greens. It was going to cover the cost, and the jobs would obviously have come in handy during the Depression. The usual tiresome boosters—the Chamber of Commerce, the politicians—were all for it. But at town meeting sessions across the state, Vermonters voted it down, telling the government to take its money and bother someone else. There already was a road along the Greens, a road for hikers.

The difference between that kind of road and the kind people are used to in their cars is the difference between reality and comfort. A hiking trail doesn't try to smooth out every hollow and soften every curve. It climbs, falls, slips, doubles back on itself. People have done countless hours of volunteer work building steps and water bars (who has ever volunteered to maintain a highway?), but even so there's inescapable mud when it rains. And inescapable effort. The effort

OPPOSITE: View of the Plains of San Agustin, New Mexico, from the Continental Divide Trail

6   ◆   AMERICA'S GREAT HIKING TRAILS

is the point. You're headed up to the hills for the joy of the effort. And so the sights you see are more beautiful than the sights that come effortlessly in through the windshield. You earn each joy.

A long hiking trail, undeniably, is therefore puritan; it exacts a toll, demands some sweat. But it's also, paradoxically, hedonistic, because after a while that toll, that sweat, becomes part of the joy. It may take a week or so while you work yourself into shape, but then you begin to become part of the rocky, sinewy path. And when that happens, when you are the trail, the adventure really begins. Effort and joy intertwine— the exact opposites of ease and pleasure that are the hallmarks of the consumer society down in the valley.

Be careful with this book, then. It will guide you to beautiful places, but also subversive and even dangerous ones. Few people have come back from one of these long hikes unchanged. These paths head north and south, east and west—but they also head, unavoidably, *in*.

INTRODUCTION

BY KAREN BERGER

What is it, I sometimes wonder, that gives a hiking trail—a mere footpath, a recreational journey, a stroll through the park, a walk in the woods—iconic status?

Say the words "Appalachian Trail" to anyone who has spent any time at all in the outdoors—summer camp, scouting, backpacking weekends—and you'll hear about dreams. They've wanted to hike it, or they've known someone who has, or, at the very least, they've done it in an armchair in company with Bill Bryson or any one of a hundred other hiker-writers who have challenged the 2,200-mile footpath with any degree of success and tried to capture it with words on paper.

Say the words "Pacific Crest" or "Continental Divide" and eyes and dreams get even bigger, with higher mountains, longer hikes, bigger vistas, and wildernesses filled with challenges and dangers: grizzly bears, summer ice slopes, endless climbs, lung-busting air.

Perhaps it is the drama of big numbers: America's 11 national scenic trails range in length from the new and relatively short 215-mile New England Trail to the behemoth 4,600-mile North Country Trail, with an average of more than 1,200 miles apiece—that's three million footsteps, more or less. We can throw more big numbers around: quantifiable boasts like biggest wilderness, highest mountain pass, longest climb. And softer, more subjective superlatives: the best views, the wildest experience, and—always worth an argument—the hardest.

Each trail has its qualities, some of them similar and some of them unique. Arizona and Florida share southern climes and wintertime accessibility, but there is no confusing the dry red sandstone buttes of

Arizona with the glistening flooded greens of Florida. One is guarded by saguaro sentinels of the desert; the other by alligators in cypress swamps. The sandy trails of the Grand Canyon are nothing like the sandy paths along the Gulf Shore beaches. Even trails that are arguably similar—say, the Pacific Crest Trail (PCT) and the Continental Divide Trail (CDT), which both power through southwestern deserts and tackle some of the tallest mountains in the contiguous 48 states—have their differences: The CDT has fewer hikers; the PCT has better-marked trail. The CDT is speckled with the remnants of American history; the PCT is revered for the iconic images of its mountain landscapes in the American wilderness movement. Each of the 11 national scenic trails has a character, a soul, if you will, and an observant hiker looking through a jumble of pictures taken on the various long-distance trails will only rarely mix them up.

Whatever the appeal, or the challenge, hikers will find it somewhere on one of America's national scenic trails. Established by Congress in 1968, and most recently updated and amended in 2009, the National Trails System Act's current language states a twofold purpose: to "provide for the ever-increasing outdoor recreation needs of an expanding population" and to "promote the preservation of, public access to, travel within, and enjoyment and appreciation of the open air." The act describes a trail system sprawling from points accessible to America's urban areas to scenic backcountry to paths along historic travel routes. It further specifies the role of volunteers in the development and maintenance of trails, and pledges to encourage and assist in these efforts. National scenic trails, the act states, "may be located so as to represent desert, marsh, grassland, mountain, canyon, river,

forest, and other areas, as well as landforms which exhibit significant characteristics of the physiographic regions of the Nation." No small mandate, that.

In all points, the act has been remarkably successful. Starting with two established national scenic trails, the National Trails System has grown to encompass 11 national scenic trails that currently wind their way through 32 states and the District of Columbia and include virtually every type of landscape in the contiguous United States. The system also includes historic trails, national recreation trails, connecting trails, and, most recently, a national geological trail, all in all covering more than 60,000 miles. It is a system that, through a combination of fierce intention and happy accident, has managed to distill the best, the most, the biggest of the American landscape— truly from redwood forests to Gulf Stream waters.

Readers of books titled some variant of *My Journey on the Great Long Hard Backpacking Trail* will recognize similarities in every long-distance attempt of any long-distance trail, even if the details and the voices are different. On one trail, the challenge may be the constant risk of dehydration and heat exhaustion; on another, the difficulty may be miles of knee-deep water. One hiker might be seeking solace and healing in the wilderness, another might be trying to set a speed record, and a third might want to find every drinking establishment within walking (or hitch-hiking) distance of the trail.

Whatever the challenge, whatever the experience sought, in the retelling, at least, the trail is always harder than promised, and the first days are always the hardest of all, with miles that are too long, weather that is too vile, insects that are too bloodthirsty, boots that are too tight, gear that is too heavy, trails that are unmarked, climbs that are too steep, and companions who are inspirational, filthy, full of character, or just plain weird. The rewards are greater too: the satisfaction of increasing fitness, the achievement of mountains climbed and obstacles overcome, the peace and solace of the wilderness, the sense of belonging to a community. All of these factor into a thru-hiker's experience, whether the trails take them over the highest peaks in the contiguous United States or through river valleys in the most populated part of the country.

Beyond the challenges, what these trails have in common is the dream. Without exception, long trails exist because someone dreamed of making connections: connections between landscapes, mountains,

historic sites, national parks, remote wildernesses, communities, and individuals. As a group, the national scenic trails offer nothing less than an outdoor diorama of the entire American landscape. Dotted with historical sites, speckled with stories, and displaying a range of ecological communities and geological formations so vast as to defy description, these 11 trails traverse or touch upon many, even most, of the nation's most iconic landscapes.

Indeed, the place-names along the routes of the national scenic trails define the American backcountry in our collective imagination. First, there are the national parks, including Yellowstone, Yosemite, Great Smoky Mountains, Mount Rainier, Crater Lake, Sequoia and Kings Canyon, Shenandoah, Rocky Mountain, Grand Canyon, Glacier, North Cascades, and Olympic—and more. There are also landscapes that don't have national-park status but are, if anything, even wilder: the Bob Marshall Wilderness, the rugged White and Green Mountains of New England, Wyoming's Wind River Mountains, the Three Sisters Wilderness in Oregon, and the Maine "wilderness" (in quotes because it's not really wilderness, but it feels like it, anyway, with the call of north-country loons echoing over shimmering ponds and the moose that drip shining droplets of water as they shake their enormous mangy heads). And just look at this list of iconic wildernesses named after legends: Ansel Adams, John Muir, William O. Douglas, and Aldo Leopold. Taken together, these are places and names that define the idea of wilderness for those who love the backcountry. They are as much a part of our American cultural identity as the Louvre is to a Parisian or the Acropolis is to a Greek.

THE VISIONARIES

Dreaming of connecting a nation's treasures by foot-trail is one thing, but turning that dream into reality is another. That is something else these trails share: they exist because of committed core groups of volunteers, often led by a seminal dreamer whose motivation, passion, and single-minded determination spanned decades of obsessive, unpaid labor.

You might think the job description of trail visionary would be an appealing one, with the rewarding task of exploring the backcountry on foot armed with a backpack, camera, GPS, maps, and notepad; gazing at mountain landscapes; and giving directions to an army of volunteers assembled to put it all in place.

OPPOSITE: Battle Axe Butte framed by chain cholla along the Arizona Trail, White Canyon Wilderness

But that pleasant image is only a small part of the job, which more often includes tedious, mind-numbing, detail-oriented paperwork, including assembling maps of landownership; collecting route information; putting together contact lists of agency managers; going through official channels at the local county, state, and federal levels; securing easements; writing management plans; building coalitions; cajoling stakeholders ranging from condominium developers to Native American tribal leaders to ranchers to town councils; reviewing management plans; and negotiating for protection from development, logging, and viewshed disruption. As much as they are passionate outdoorspeople, trail visionaries must be paper pushers, negotiators, bullies, inspirational preachers, salesmen, analysts, politicians, and fund-raisers.

From the hiker's trailside viewpoint, the work of trail visionaries, clubs, and volunteers may not at first be obvious. We hikers can be a nearsighted bunch. On our first forays, we are in awe of the scenery and in agony with our blisters; we often don't stop to consider who actually put the trail we are walking on underfoot, except, perhaps, to curse the trail maintainers when we lose the way or when the trail takes a particularly gnarly path uphill.

But the more time we spend on trails, the more apt we are to consider aspects of hiking beyond pack weight and blisters and how far it is to the next water source. We start appreciating trail amenities: blazes so carefully repainted, poison ivy cut back, trail shelters repaired, fire rings cleared, latrines cleaned, water bars placed to drain water off the trail, and rock ledges placed so carefully one might think for a moment they were put there by the same great forces that raised the mountains and carved the canyons. It becomes obvious, once we look beyond our own two feet, that the view from the mountain peak is truly the tip of an iceberg, and that the paths on which we walk are held up not only by geology, but by a mountain of paperwork, an eternity of volunteer hours, and lifetimes of labors of love.

Indeed, this groundswell of popular support and volunteer hours makes the long-distance trails system something unique in the bureaucracy of government-supported federal projects: it is a grassroots-generated effort. All the formality of designation and official routes and certified trails and government oversight agencies came after the fact. That the importance and primacy of volunteers are recognized up front in the

OPPOSITE: The North Country Trail to Old Man's Cave, Hocking Hills State Park, Ohio

formal language of the National Trails System Act is a testament that the trails could not exist without the people who love them.

That spirit is at the heart of the national scenic trails, present at the very beginning. The Appalachian Trail (AT)—the granddaddy of the National Scenic Trails System—did not begin in the office of some nameless government agency. It began with one man sitting on one mountain, thinking about the value of wilderness in an increasingly industrial age and considering how a trail through wild lands close to urban centers might protect both the land and the soul of the American worker. That Benton MacKaye's vision showed up so clearly in the law that 50 years later finally protected the Appalachian and Pacific Crest Trails and established the framework for others shows the power of an idea.

Credit must be given: the idea of long trails was not new, and the AT was not the first. New England already had a long-distance trail—Vermont's Long Trail was established in 1910, a full decade before the AT became a topic of conversation in trail clubs and around campfires. What was new was the all-encompassing vision of a long-distance hiking trail being more than recreational, being somehow important to the spiritual and physical health of a nation. A 14-state footpath that linked the most scenic points of the highest, wildest lands was something on a different order of magnitude, and the idea of a long-distance trail spread from person to person across the country like an Internet virus—although at the slower rate of an analog world.

Local trail organizations joined the effort, offering to incorporate existing segments of their trails in the new system. Volunteers pushed unicycle-like measuring wheels over thousands of miles of terrain, including rocks, mud, and mountains. Organizations formed. The Civilian Conservation Corps (CCC) of the Depression era was called out to the woods, and built long, swinging, beautifully switchbacked trails that were so well engineered that they have clung to their precipitous hillsides for a century, defying gravity and water and the tread of millions of boots. In the spirit of "if you build it, they will come," volunteers built the AT and the hikers did, indeed, come: first in a trickle, then in a stream, and finally in rivers that today occasionally test the resources of the trail's most popular areas.

And the idea kept spreading, far beyond the Appalachians. Unable to be contained within the mountains of the east, it jumped clear across the country to the behemoth western ranges of the Sierras and Cascades. The Pacific Crest Trail's path from idea to reality took a similar course, traveling first through the minds of visionaries, then coordinating with local clubs to use portions of existing routes, such as the John Muir Trail in the High Sierra and the Cascade Crest Trail in Washington, and then doing new work on the ground with the aid of volunteers such as the Boy Scouts.

So while the National Trails System Act of 1968 didn't invent the idea of long-distance hiking trails, it did acknowledge that the Appalachian Trail and the Pacific Crest Trail already existed, and that they were big enough and important enough to be protected on a federal level. It also saw that there would be constituencies for more trails, and that these trails, too, would need protection and funding and organization and management. As importantly, it set up a framework for encouraging similar trails to be developed and a process by which they could be incorporated into the system.

The Appalachian and Pacific Crest Trails received the first formal designations in the 1968 National Trails System Act. Fourteen more trails were listed for study and possible inclusion in the system, of which four—the Continental Divide Trail, the Natchez Trace Trail, the Potomac Heritage Trail, and the North Country Trail—were certified as national scenic trails over the next 15 years. Some of the other trails on the study list became national historic trails, a category created in 1978 to protect and highlight historic American routes of travel, such as the Iditarod Trail and the Oregon Trail. The Ice Age Trail joined the national scenic trails roster in 1980, the Florida Trail joined in 1983, and in 2009, the New England Trail, the Arizona Trail, and the Pacific Northwest Trail became the most recent additions to the list.

And so we have a system of 11 national scenic trails covering more than 18,000 miles of the American landscape ("approximately" is the best we can do, as not all the trails are finished, and not all the routes are finalized), each reflecting a different aspect of America's ecology, environment, rural culture, geology, and scenery. And we have an additional 19 national historic trails that delve into and showcase America's past. In some cases, we have trails that could easily be in either category, because they offer so much of both backcountry recreation and historic interpretation. The system also includes national recreation trails, which range in length from less than a half mile to many hundreds of miles—more than 1,200 of them, offering recreation experiences ranging from hiking to biking to kayaking and canoeing to running to horseback riding to skiing to motorized use.

As a result, this trail system, which began with two hiking trails nearly 50 years ago, may offer the best way to see and understand America: to know its geological and environmental diversity, to see how a small town in South Dakota is the same and yet different from a small town in Massachusetts, and to follow in the footsteps of colonial pioneers, emigrant trail settlers, gold rush panners, beaver trappers, Native Americans, Civil War fighters, and railroad and empire builders. These trails show us the iconic landscapes that inspired the pioneers of the American wilderness movement. They preserve for us and for future generations the experience of the sheer magnitude of the diversity of the American landscape.

This is not to say that every mile of every trail is spectacular in the traditional sense of high mountains and scenic vistas. But every trail *is* interesting, with its own special view into its part of the patchwork of the American landscape. The high peaks of California, the grizzly-inhabited north country of Montana, the weirdly sculpted glacial formations of Wisconsin, the swamps of Florida, the fierce drylands and deserts of Arizona: all these trails showcase very different notions of beauty spots and points of interest. They also serve different needs and populations. Some answer our need for wild remote lonesome high points; others offer islands of backcountry respite to residents of nearby populated communities. And, as one might expect of trails that connect one high point—literally or figuratively—to another, the sometimes long miles in between can be more or less interesting, with unfinished sections that weekend and short-term hikers will happily skip, but that long-distance hikers hoping to claim completion must muscle through.

THE VOLUNTEERS

Volunteers built most of the National Scenic Trails System blaze by blaze, and their job is ongoing and unending. The community of supporters, donors, and volunteers varies by trail, depending on local enthusiasm, outreach efforts, how well established the trail is, and the population base. Perhaps the best example of the effect of volunteerism on a trail is found on the

OPPOSITE: The Appalachian Trail along Hall Mountain, Maine

Appalachian Trail, blessed with a long history and a location that is an easy drive from most of the big eastern metropolitan areas. AT volunteers number in the tens of thousands—the AT even has its very own museum, its own land trust, and biennial member conferences. What this means for hikers is that guide-books and maps are plentiful, updated, and accurate; Internet chat rooms are lively; and on-trail events are common and well attended.

On other trails, volunteerism varies. In more densely populated areas, tight groups of local main-tainers are often found. On more remote sections of more remote trails, volunteers may be spread too thin, but trail clubs sometimes offer backcoun-try working "vacations" to bring volunteers to areas in need of trail work. More volunteers mean better trail maintenance, better organization of volunteer work, more frequently updated guidebooks, and better access to information about trail conditions. Well-organized trail-management clubs ensure that information about problems—flooding, blowdowns, ice-storm damage, washouts—quickly reaches trail-maintenance groups, which pick up their Pulaskis and shovels and either fix the problem or report back with recommendations for relocations.

On trails with still-unfinished segments, infor-mation may be harder to find, especially in remote areas. Fewer volunteers and maintainers may be on the job. On remote sections of the Continental Divide Trail, for example, it may be several years before a segment that has been destroyed by forest fire is relo-cated. Cross-country and navigational skills can be essential for both hikers and volunteer maintainers.

CHOOSING A TRAIL

So how to choose which trail to hike? For most people, a weekend backpacking trip is a big adven-ture, a two-week hiking vacation is a very big deal, a two-month summer hike falls into the category of a major luxury, and a six-month thru-hike is an almost unimaginable dream.

Long-distance hikers planning to spend several weeks or months on a trail should consider a vari-ety of factors: drama, scenery, ecosystem diversity, the quality and difficulty of the trail, maintenance, opportunities for social interaction with other hik-ers, convenience of access and resupply, historical sites, geological sites, wilderness values, crowds, the presence or absence of regulations, and wildlife.

OPPOSITE: Spruce trees reflected in a pond along the Continental Divide Trail, Park Range, Routt National Forest, Colorado

Bragging rights also factor in, sometimes involving length, difficulty, and whether a hiker can claim to be the "first" to do something: the fastest, the first woman, the first family, the first person to hike the trail both ways, or—who knows?—even the first to do a trail on a pogo stick.

For short-term hikers out for only a weekend or a few days, access may be a more important issue: The Appalachian Trail, for example, is within a two-hour drive of most of the major cities in the eastern metropolis from Maine to Georgia. The New England Trail is a quick drive from all of southern and central New England, as well as the New York metropolitan area. Some of the North Country Trail is within a convenient hop of many of the northern Midwest urban centers, including much of the states of Ohio and Michigan. The frequent road crossings that intersect these trails make getting to them more convenient than traveling to many sections of a more remote trail, such as the Continental Divide, where many trail sections are long drives from major western cities, and where trail access may require an expedition in a four-wheel-drive vehicle on a dirt road to the middle of nowhere.

In between the two extremes of weekend hikers and long-distance backpackers are the vacation backpackers: hikers with a week or two or three, a time frame that might justify a long drive or a plane trip. For these hikers, choosing a trail is all about the scenery and the drama, considered in tandem with concerns about climate, season, bugs, water availability, and trail conditions.

This book will help you plan the hike of your dreams, whether it's a peaceful voyage in your armchair, a short walk close to home, or a six-month wilderness adventure. In each chapter, we focus on describing, through words and photography, each of the national scenic trails, searching for something in its essential character that makes it unique: its soul, if you will. For each trail, we include information about its route and its history, along with highlights and beauty spots for hikers seeking trips of various durations. But more importantly, we try to illustrate the combination of factors—landscape, communities, geology, environment, land use, history—that gives each trail its own special accent, its own window in the kaleidoscope that is the American backcountry.

As for the future, the list of national scenic trails is nowhere near complete. Though the challenges involved in proposing and creating a new national scenic trail are daunting, trails are still being built, constructed, and linked together, fueled by the visions of dreamers who look to the next horizon and then the one after that. The list has been slowly growing since 1968 when the first two trails were designated. We are confident that it will continue to grow.

Standing in the wings—on deck, as it were—is a network of other spectacular American trails, some of which may eventually find their way onto this list, and some of which would add other ecosystems, landscapes, histories, and communities to the mix. The last chapter in this book takes a look at these important trails, some of which—such as the Hawaii's Kalalau Trail on Kauai's Napali Coast, Alaska's Chilkoot Trail, California's John Muir Trail, and Vermont's Long Trail—have iconic histories of their own.

There is something about trails that go beyond the horizon that captures the imagination. Somehow, being part of these long trails matters, even to people who don't intend to walk more than a couple of miles to a waterfall and back. Perhaps it is the appeal of the unknown adventure waiting beyond the next rise, or the allure of a viewpoint just out of sight. Perhaps it is the knowledge that we are walking in a line of footsteps that extends back through generations. Perhaps it is simply being part of something so big. We may find ourselves on day hikes, unable or unwilling to turn back. And once in a while, we might turn the dream of continuing on and on and on into reality.

In the so-called "Wilderness Letter" to the Outdoor Recreation Resources Review Commission (1960), American writer Wallace Stegner once wrote:

> We need wilderness preserved—as much of it as is still left, and as many kinds—because it was the challenge against which our character as a people was formed. The reminder and the reassurance that it is still there is good for our spiritual health even if we never once in ten years set foot in it. It is good for us when we are young, because of the incomparable sanity it can bring briefly, as vacation and rest, into our insane lives. It is important to us when we are old simply because it is there—important, that is, simply as an idea.

Perhaps it's the same with long trails: we need to know that they continue beyond the horizon, even if we never once set foot there.

OPPOSITE: Cascades along Briggs Brook on the Metacomet-Monadnack Trail section of the New England Trail, Massachusetts

THE APPALACHIAN TRAIL

➤ COMMUNITY IN THE WILDERNESS ◄

What is it about the Appalachian Trail? • As outdoor icons go, the Appalachian Trail (AT) is the outdoorsperson's Holy Grail. Anyone with the slightest interest in such things has heard of it. Hiking it gets placed on bucket lists alongside trekking the Himalayas or climbing Kilimanjaro. Having completed all of its nearly 2,200 miles gives a backpacker immediate street cred in the been-there-done-that world of outdoor one-upmanship. People connect with the dream. • A modest green tunnel, the Appalachian Trail is overwhelmingly a forested path with only occasional jaunts above the tree line. Parallel to America's thickly populated Eastern Seaboard, it is rarely more than a two- or three-hour drive from major cities like Boston, New York, Washington, and Atlanta. Its highest point doesn't even reach 7,000 feet. • It has views, yes, and beauty spots, but far more often, the Appalachian Trail winds through closed-in forests that offer no competition to the alpine spectacles of the Continental Divide Trail, the red-rock pinnacles of the Arizona Trail, or the old-growth forests of the Pacific Northwest Trail. It is not the oldest long trail in America (that honor goes to Vermont's Long Trail). It is not even in the running for being the longest trail. And although the grand old man of long-distance trails can still pack a punch—gnarly footways, rocky scrambles, late-spring blackflies, ridiculous extremes of temperature, and absurd routes that head straight uphill, incline be damned—he's far from the toughest dude on the long-distance hiking block.

No matter. This is the trail that people choose for their trip of a lifetime. Each year, thousands of people declare their intention to hike the entire Appalachian Trail. By contrast, between 500 and 800 are estimated to try the Pacific Crest Trail each year, and the Continental Divide Trail might attract a couple dozen hopefuls in a good year. The number of prospective thru-hikers on most other national scenic trails rarely crawls into double digits.

WHY THE APPALACHIAN TRAIL?

It's no use trying to figure out the magic of the trail from a distance: the answers waft along on ridges, murmur along rivers, echo across north-country lakes, or whisper on the wind of rocky peaks. For example: Let's take a fairly typical stretch of trail, from Lions Head to Jug End ridge near the Connecticut-Massachusetts border. A rocky outcropping juts out, breaking apart the forest curtain of upland pitch pine and mountain laurel. It is one of a series of scenic overlooks where you can step away from the ridgeline trail and survey the Housatonic River Valley to the east. The broad floodplain edged by low mountains encapsulates what may be a microcosm of the Appalachian Trail, a postcard-perfect patchwork of forests, hills, cornfields, ponds, farms, streams, and swampy grasslands that edge the river. The outcropping is a good place to rest, to eat lunch, to take a photo—and to ponder just what it is that makes this seemingly modest green tunnel one of the world's most iconic hiking destinations.

From on high, the answer isn't immediately evident, although no one would argue that the view isn't pretty. But it isn't dramatic, either. Rather, it is a typical view on the Appalachian Trail: lots of green, contours that hide more contours, a hint of farms and towns, and another ridge to climb on the other side.

After a period of heavy rain, the Housatonic River below the ridge sometimes floods. Looking to the lowlands, the observant hiker might see glints of sunlight reflecting on water where no water should be. The hiker who is familiar with the route ahead knows that it is subject to flooding and that the vernal pools will be full of water.

In the vernal pools—think of them as marshy sponges that can be trusted neither for reliable year-round water nor for a solid dry place to walk—semi-aquatic species that can survive a dry spell live alongside terrestrial species that don't mind being submerged for a while. The swampy areas in the river valley are prone to flooding, so puncheons—rough-hewn log planks—protect fragile vegetation by giving hikers a place to walk, while trees mix with water lilies, and beavers remake the landscape. In either the pool or the swamp, a hiker might see water-loving salamanders and frogs, forest-loving moose, and swamp-loving muskrats, not to mention the catfish that, in times of flooding, have been known to take a wrong turn and swim down the trail.

The vernal pool and the swampy trail are ecotones, places where different and sometimes contradictory ecological communities intersect: wet and dry; field and forest; upland and lowland. Species that live in either of the two distinct ecological zones find their way here, and a new environment is formed, which attracts species of its own along with the usual opportunists—white-tailed deer, black bears, coyotes, poison ivy, mosquitoes—that seem to thrive everywhere. The resulting community is rich and unique, more, and different, than the sum of its parts.

The same can be said of the Appalachian Trail. The intersection of conflicting ideas is as bred into the DNA of the AT as it is in the muddy waters of a vernal pool. And the answer to the question—What makes the Appalachian Trail the big kahuna, the iconic image, the trail everyone knows?—might be found in this simple ecological concept. The AT is a place where seemingly incompatible elements—humans and wilderness, towns and trails, solitude and community—come together to create something found nowhere else. It is a mature ecotone, nourished by time and tradition. And as such, it is unique in the world of long-distance hiking.

THE STORY OF A DREAM

In a very real sense, the Appalachian Trail was founded on the idea of contradiction. It was also a product of the challenges, opportunities, and developing wilderness philosophies of its time and place.

The time was the turn of the last century. The place was the Eastern Seaboard, home to the quickly industrializing cities of the eastern metropolis and the still-wild Appalachian Mountains that framed them to the west.

Most long-distance trails begin with a dreamer, and the Appalachian Trail is no exception. According to trail legend—and who wants to mess with a good yarn?—the Appalachian Trail dream began on another New England overlook.

Somewhere—the dreamer referred to here later vaguely recalled that it might have been in the White Mountains of New Hampshire—a young man gazes out over a sea of rolling peaks and imagines a footpath that connects one to the next and the one after that. Fed by bracing mountain air, unfettered by inconvenient practicalities such as money and land-ownership and legalities, the dream grows and the imagined path continues past the horizon, winding

its way over every natural beauty spot in the still-wild Appalachian Corridor, through 14 states from Maine to Georgia.

Benton MacKaye was this dreamer. The first graduate of Harvard University's then-new forestry program, a cofounder of a progressive politics group known as the hell-raisers, and a regional planner, MacKaye is painted by biographers as part Renaissance man, part social idealist, and part impractical dreamer.

Perhaps not *that* impractical. By some accounts, more than a decade passed between those early New England hikes and any real action, but in 1921, MacKaye wrote an article for the *Journal of the American Institute of Architects*. Titled "An Appalachian Trail: A Project in Regional Planning," MacKaye's article proposed "a 'long trail' over the full length of the Appalachian skyline, from the highest peak in the north to the highest peak in the south—from Mt. Washington to Mt. Mitchell."

It is neither incidental nor accidental that MacKaye presented his idea in a journal for architects rather than land managers. His Appalachian Trail was intended not as mere recreation, but as a response to increasing urbanization, which he felt threatened the health of both landscapes and humans. And grand as his proposal for a 2,000-mile wilderness trail was, it was also only one part of a grander idea involving camps and communities that would offer a therapeutic wilderness response to modern life, balm for the souls of armies of happy factory workers who would cheerfully trudge up and down mountains doing physical activities that were rejuvenating and healthful. (One can only wonder what he would make of the modern concept of weekend rejuvenation, with so much time spent on couches in front of television sets watching other people run up and down a field.)

MacKaye's idea for an Appalachian Trail may have been ambitious, huge, even ridiculous, but it was fully in keeping with the gestalt of its time. Coming a mere decade after the Theodore Roosevelt administration—which saw the founding of the United States Forest Service—and on the heels of the formation of the National Park Service, Benton MacKaye's idea was bookended by the work of earlier and later giants of the conservation movement, such as John Muir and Ansel Adams. MacKaye sat in meetings with grand men with grand ideas about grand landscapes, informed by new policies and philosophies

about wilderness. It was a crucible that would create a framework for conservation and what it means to a modern world.

MacKaye saw the Appalachian Mountains as the last bulwark against the encroachment of civilization on the eastern part of the American continent, a battle line announcing that the smoky cities could pass no farther. And today's trail along the ridges of the highest and wildest country east of the Mississippi River does, indeed, act as an antidote to congestion and stress and pollution and traffic and digital addiction—whether that relief lasts a half day or an entire hiking season.

The Appalachian Trail is the only part of MacKaye's plan that came into fruition: there are no happy work camps of urban escapees restoring their inner balance with the joys of tilling the land, no primitive public camps with chop-your-own-firewood and haul-your-own-water (unless you count the campgrounds for RVs with satellite dishes and Wi-Fi hookups). What there is, is a long green tunnel. But, in a way that MacKaye did not envision, the Appalachian Trail has become a community in the wilderness—and the antidote to contemporary life that he imagined a century ago.

FOOTPATH THROUGH THE WILDERNESS

Like any other hiking trail, the Appalachian Trail is defined, at least in part, by its wildness. But today's Appalachians are much tamer than the mountains Benton MacKaye gazed upon. Today, eastern wilderness is to some extent an oxymoron. While for most of the year the thick Appalachian foliage creates an illusion of isolation, in winter the truth emerges between the stark brown branches of deciduous forest. On a clear night, civilization twinkles far below the ridges, clearly visible: blue fluorescent streetlamps, tallow yellow house lights, and the tiny white headlamps of cars winding along a valley road. Even in its most remote and rugged locations, most of the land has been at some time farmed or logged and most of the large predators have been exterminated (although black bears and coyotes have made a significant comeback in recent years). No matter where you are on the trail, you are likely to pass some evidence of human habitation: the lone big out-of-scale trees in a forest were probably planted to establish property lines 200 years ago; stone walls on a mountain side were put there to mark boundaries, to fence in sheep, or simply to store rocks cleared for farming;

the ruins of a whiskey still may molder in a "holler." The amount of true wilderness—unsettled, untrammeled—has shrunk since MacKaye's day.

As beautiful, dramatic, grand, and, yes, even wild as the Appalachian Trail may be, it is never far from a road, or a town, or, for that matter, from help, which undermines, if only a little, the hiker's self-image as a rugged conqueror of wilderness challenges. Instead, the Appalachian Trail is a hiking path that is within a one-day drive of more than two-thirds of the population of the United States. It is three hours from Pittsburgh. Two hours from Boston. An hour from New York City. A little more than that from Philadelphia, Atlanta, or Washington, DC. On the Appalachian Trail, the idea of wilderness collides with the reality of populated urban America, and the result is its own kind of ecotone: a new and unique environment, much richer than the sum of its parts.

And for most visitors, the Appalachian Trail is wild enough: access and civilization notwithstanding, you can die out there, from heart-attack-inducing climbs, hypothermia (yes, in August), falls, drownings, the extremely rare bear attack, and the only slightly more common attack by human predators. Go to the top of Mount Washington—yes, the one with the road, the restaurant, the weather station, and the cog railway—on a late September day when the barometer has plummeted like a rock fall, the rain is blowing sideways, the fog is as thick as a hiker's morning oatmeal, and you've hiked a few miles away from the safety of the summit house. You might then have cause to consider the list of all the people—more than 120 as of this writing—who have died up there. Hikers like to claim that you are safer on the Appalachian Trail than in your own neighborhood, and depending on the statistics they use, not to mention your backcountry skills and the neighborhood you live in, they may be right. But the unfamiliar wildness of wilderness—designated or not—adds the amplifying aspect of a sense of risk.

THRU-HIKERS AND TRAIL COMMUNITY

Wild or not, the Appalachian Trail is also a community—of hikers, volunteers, trail officials, lawyers, environmentalists, politicians, and land managers. And how that community interacts with the trail, the wilderness, the towns through which the trail passes, and each other, gives the AT its special flavor, its identity, its iconic status.

That special flavor has changed a great deal in the last two decades. According to the Appalachian Trail Conservancy, the umbrella organization that coordinates maintenance and management of the trail, some two to three million people a year hike on the AT—whether for an hour or a season. The number is of necessity a guesstimate: no one is standing at the hundreds of road crossings taking notes when a local resident strolls out for a morning walk or a weekend backpacker hoists a load and strides uphill.

Among these millions are two to three thousand ambitious dreamers who annually declare their intention to hike the whole thing from Georgia to Maine (or, less often, the other way). These are the thru-hikers: a small minority of trail users with a huge presence. In the last two decades, their numbers have exploded.

The Appalachian Trail Conservancy keeps records of those who report having hiked the entire trail, either in one continuous hike, or—even more rarely—in a series of hikes over several years. As of this writing, some 13,600 have reported completing hikes of the entire length of the Appalachian Trail, either in one massive hike (five million steps, give or take, five months, ditto, and some 500,000 feet of elevation gain) or in multiple hikes (the same miles and climbs spread out over several years). Of those 13,600 hikers, 8,000 have completed their hikes since the year 2000, compared to approximately 5,600 in the seven previous decades combined. The rising numbers have been fueled by publicity and books about the trail, most notably travel writer Bill Bryson's *A Walk in the Woods*, a hilarious account of a spectacularly failed thru-hike attempt. The completion percentage, however, has stayed low: the ATC estimates that about 70 percent of thru-hikers do not complete the journey.

Any way you look at it, the raw number of thru-hikers is a small group, but compressed onto a narrow trail, traveling together in the same seasons, it's big enough for an entire culture to have formed, with its own language and traditions and accepted customs, etiquette, and rules. There are trail celebrities and trail pariahs, trail names and trail celebrations. The hiker thinking that a springtime weekend walk on the southern portion of the Appalachian Trail will offer solitude and the company of only an occasional bird or shelter mouse is in for a surprise. With 40, 50, 60, or even more hikers starting a thru-hike on any given spring day, shelters are not only full, they are surrounded by tent cities. Names are exchanged—not the prosaic Janes and Bobs of everyday life, but fanciful monikers like Rockhopper and Carnivore, Dirty Harry and Iron Lady. The adoption of a trail name indicates a walking away from everyday life, a new persona, an acceptance into the thru-hiker community, and maybe even a rejection of what went before.

There are two ways to look at this vibrant growing community. On one hand there is the magic of interaction between people of all walks of life. Virtually every facet of American society is represented on the trail, though not proportionately: men outnumber women, and African Americans, Hispanic Americans, and Asian Americans account for only a miniscule number of thru-hikers. But all professions and ages, from prekindergartner to octogenarian, have tried their feet at thru-hiking. Occupations include everything from government workers to veterans to professors to doctors to lawyers to housewives to out-of-work college dropouts. For such disparate people—often separated by socioeconomic barriers in "real life"—the ability to interact easily is one of the real gifts of the trail.

On the other hand, the popularity of the trail has led to some overcrowding, particularly in the midst of the thru-hiking season, which has changed the dynamic between hikers and the backcountry. Like a river overflowing its banks, the number of long-distance hikers sometimes seems to be stressing the relationships between hikers and the communities through which they pass, and between hikers and each other. The trail's reputation as a retreat from society, a place of freedom in the wilderness, has morphed into a different animal, more Bonnie and Clyde than John Muir. The moniker "hiker trash" used to be given in jest to thru-hikers; now it seems to be accurately descriptive of a small but visible subset of hikers. There is more graffiti, more garbage, more late-night partying. At times, the spring northbound thru-hiking season appears to be one unmanageable frat party. Like most frat parties, this one is fun only for those who choose to be there.

As a result, those looking for an actual nature-oriented, meditative hiking experience might avoid the southernmost 450 miles of the trail, from Springer Mountain to Damascus, Virginia, in spring, and head instead to Maine. A southbound start from the trail's Maine terminus offers a completely different

PREVIOUS SPREAD: The AT through Sinking Creek Valley, Washington-Jefferson National Forest, Virginia (left); McAfee Knob, Washington-Jefferson National Forest, Virginia

OPPOSITE: AT hiker near Boiling Springs, Pennsylvania (top); Delaware Water Gap from Mount Tammany, New Jersey (bottom)

experience. After the climb of Katahdin, the first hundred miles go through a relatively inaccessible wilderness stretch where opportunities to portage in beer and pop out to hiker festivals and town bars are few and far between. The next stretch, through western Maine, is the most difficult on the entire trail. It can take all day to hike 10 miles over boulders the size of elephants. It's not the easy way to start—but it offers more backcountry and nature, less partying and community. As thru-hikers are fond of saying, "Hike your own hike."

Running parallel with the hiker community is another community, one that stays in the background as the flashy, ephemeral hikers pass through. The Appalachian towns through which the AT passes have come to an understanding with their peripatetic seasonal neighbors. Some towns are matter-of-fact about the trail, happy enough to take hiker dollars in exchange for supplies and a hotel room, but they otherwise remain uninvolved. Many towns, however, have become part of the trail fabric, some with hostels, others with hiker gatherings or church suppers open to hikers. "Trail angels" in some trail towns dispense "trail magic"—hosting hikers in their homes, giving rides to hikers bound for town stops, or unexpectedly wining and dining hikers with anything from a cold bottle of soda to a full-fledged on-trail barbecue. Some towns have entire festivals devoted to hikers, one of which—"Trail Days" in Damascus, Virginia—attracts some 20,000 hikers past and present into town for slide shows, gear demonstrations, and socializing. The town beauty queen is crowned Miss Appalachian Trail, and rides in sequined splendor in the parade down Main Street. The hikers march, too.

Perhaps most important to the existence of the trail, however, are the builders and maintainers—both professionals and volunteers. Without them, the trail wouldn't have been built, it wouldn't have been protected by Congress, and it wouldn't exist today.

If Benton MacKaye's ideals speak to the soul of a thru-hiker—escaping from the mainstream, rejecting the industrial monolith, healing and rejuvenating in the backcountry—it is a different man who speaks to the hearts of the maintainers, many of whom have contributed decades of service. Benton MacKaye might have been the dreamer who envisioned the trail, but to put it on the ground required not merely dreams but brute force, and in this, the dreamer was overtaken by the doer: dynamic Myron Avery,

who trudged the entire length of the trail pushing a measuring wheel up and down rocks, over boulders, and across swamps to take exact measurements from point to point. The human partnership—some might say nonpartnership—between MacKaye and Avery was every bit as disparate as the ideas that had launched the trail, but between the inspiration and idealism of the one and the practical organization of the other, the trail had what it needed. That's another contradiction in the ecotone, illustrated by the contrast between the grubby, shaggy thru-hikers and the settled communities of maintainers whose commitment to the trail tallies up to many thousands of hours.

So, to return to the original question: What is it about the Appalachian Trail?

Perhaps it is simply its core contradictions that create its magic: community with wilderness, long-distance hikers with trail towns, government with private partnerships, a thin corridor of wilderness through the most populated part of America. The ever-shifting balance of hikers, volunteers, communities, trail angels, alumni, professional land managers, and temporary celebrities who each year become the oldest, youngest, fastest, or slowest to hike the AT form the mosaic of a trail that is, in the end, much more than a trail—as it was always envisioned to be.

THE ROUTE

All the official trail literature—including the National Trails System Act and the trail's own motto, which since 1923 has been "Maine to Georgia"—describes the Appalachian Trail as starting at Katahdin in Maine and going south to Georgia, but out of deference to the vast majority of thru-hikers who "walk with spring" and go the other way, the description here joins them and heads north.

The southern section of the trail comprises Georgia, North Carolina, and Tennessee. These are hefty mountains—four, five, and six thousand feet high, with many miles of switchbacks swinging this way and that. Much of the trail follows the North Carolina-Tennessee border.

Starting on Springer Mountain in northwest Georgia near the old gold-mining town of Dahlonega, the trail begins with a no-nonsense introduction to the AT's characteristic ups and downs. It crosses into North Carolina near the Nantahala River, and then heads up into the Stekoahs, through what is generally

The Appalachian Trail

Approximately 2,200 miles from Maine to Georgia

N

Maine

Presque Isle

Bangor

Augusta

Belfast

Montpelier

VT

NH

Portland

Hanover

Killington

Concord

Glens Falls

New York

Boston

Syracuse

Mass

Albany

Springfield

Buffalo

Hartford

RI

Binghamton

Conn

Erie

Sunbury

New York

Michigan

Newark

Cleveland

Pennsylvania

Philadelphia

Trenton

Akron

Harrisburg

NJ

Atlantic City

Pittsburgh

Ohio

MD

Columbus

Harpers Ferry

Dover

Washington, DC

Del

West Virginia

Charleston

Richmond

Virginia

Lexington

Hampton

Lynchburg

Kentucky

Durham

Winston-Salem

Raleigh

North Carolina

Jacksonville

Tennessee

Charlotte

Greenville

Wilmington

Dahlonega

Columbia

Georgia

South Carolina

Augusta

APPALACHIAN TRAIL

AT

NATIONAL SCENIC TRAIL

— The Appalachian Trail

— Interstate Highway

0   25 miles   50 miles   100 miles   150 miles   200 miles

considered one of the rougher and steeper sections of the trail. Next, the trail hugs the North Carolina-Tennessee border on the crest of Great Smoky Mountains National Park, and continues along the border through a series of difficult, steep climbs over the Southern Balds (Roan Mountain, Big Bald, Little Bald, and Max Patch are a few of the notable peaks). It then stays in Tennessee before entering Virginia. During this first 450 miles, about half of the intended thru-hikers drop out.

The Virginia section of the trail (along with a short foray along the West Virginia border near the New River and again just south of Harpers Ferry and the Potomac River) comprises nearly a quarter of the entire trail. With gentler grades, it is generally considered some of the easiest trail, and thru-hikers often average well above 20 miles a day. However, "easy" is in the eyes (or legs and lungs) of the beholder; it is not unreasonable to conclude that the Virginia portion of the AT seems easy only because of what came before. The trail loosely parallels Interstate 81 on a southwest-to-northeast course through the state, and also follows near and frequently crosses both the Blue Ridge Parkway and Skyline Drive in Shenandoah National Park. Just shy of the halfway point, the trail briefly enters West Virginia (home of the Appalachian Trail headquarters in historic Harpers Ferry, an important Civil War historic site), and then makes a quick foray into Maryland before reaching the halfway point in southern Pennsylvania, where the Appalachian Trail Museum commemorates everything from early hiking equipment to contemporary ecology.

Pennsylvania is a landscape formed by glaciation, and in this particular case, what that means to hikers is that there are rocks—millions and millions of rocks, rolling underfoot, grabbing at toes, sliding, ankle-twisting. The grades are not usually excessively steep, but the glacial debris makes for difficult walkways. Hikers call it Rocksylvania.

The remaining states in the mid-Atlantic pass quickly: New Jersey—entered at the Delaware Water Gap—is prettier than hikers expect it to be, especially on ridges framed by early summer mountain laurel. New York is characterized by the farms and fields of the Hudson Valley, small, increasingly developed communities, and smallish mountains, although appearances can be deceptive: by going up and down every bump in the vicinity it is possible to climb a good 5,000 feet in a solid day of hiking, even if the elevation of the tallest mountain barely caps 1,000 feet.

If the trail in New Jersey and New York is surprising, the trail in Connecticut is a revelation, starting with a lovely walk along and above the Housatonic River, and followed by an ascent of the ridges of northern Connecticut and southern Massachusetts, still overlooking the Housatonic. After entering Massachusetts, the trail dips east to cross the Housatonic floodplain, and ascends the other side, now fully in the Massachusetts Berkshires, where it will stay until it reaches the state high point at Mount Greylock, just shy of the Vermont border.

The trail in Vermont is at first contiguous with its inspiration: it follows Vermont's Long Trail for about 100 miles, then, near Killington, it swings east toward New Hampshire. Entering New Hampshire in Hanover, the trail becomes increasingly higher, wilder, rockier, and more difficult, with the climb and descent of Mount Moosilauke announcing full-fledged arrival in all the spectacle and difficulty of the White Mountains. Much of the hiking here is exposed, dramatically above the tree line, and very, very difficult, often requiring as much rock scrambling as walking. Indeed, this section, followed by the first 90 miles of Maine, is not only the most difficult of the Appalachian Trail; it is the most difficult of the entire National Scenic Trails System.

Maine ups the ante shortly after hikers cross the state line: steep-sided rock-strewn Mahoosuc Notch is known as the "toughest mile on the Appalachian Trail." It is less a hike than a scramble through an obstacle course of fallen rocks ranging from the size of pebbles to elephants with the occasional motor-home-sized rock tilted sideways with white blazes painted up the sides. The scrambling continues on and off (and up and down) for the next 90 miles. The penultimate section of the trail, the Maine Wilderness is a much easier 100-mile stretch—a respite from all the work gone before and, with its wilderness character, north-country ponds, and deep-north woods, a fitting section leading up to the reward: the final ascent of Katahdin.

OPPOSITE: Beaver Brook, White Mountain National Forest, New Hampshire

FOLLOWING SPREAD: Suspension bridge over the Peabody River, White Mountains, New Hampshire (top left); an AT hiker on Mount Height, White Mountains, New Hampshire (bottom left); the AT heading toward Lake of the Clouds, White Mountains, New Hampshire (right)

OPPOSITE: View from East
Peak of Baldpate Mountain,
Mahoosuc Range, Maine

RIGHT: The AT along Bemis
Mountain, Bemis Range, Maine

FOLLOWING SPREAD: A hiker
crossing Orbeton Stream,
Maine (top left); young
bull moose, Baxter State
Park, Maine (middle left);
Rainbow Stream lean-to,
100-Mile Wilderness, Maine
(bottom left); Mount Katahdin
reflected in West Branch of
Penobscot River, Maine (right)

APPALACHIAN TRAIL

The Appalachian Trail offers day hikers, weekend hikers, and short-term hikers an abundance of choices because it crosses back roads on a fairly frequent basis, allowing hikers to select hikes of varying lengths. Yet, at the same time, the trail offers several sections of intense multiday backcountry experience, as in the Smoky Mountains, the White Mountains, and the 100-Mile Wilderness of central Maine.

SPRINGER MOUNTAIN APPROACH TRAIL (Georgia)

You're not even on the Appalachian Trail until you've completed the 8.8-mile approach trail from Amicalola Falls State Park, but this famous climb—immortalized in Bill Bryson's book, *A Walk in the Woods*—is a must-do on the AT. A more viewful hike in the same part of the state is Blood Mountain, about 40 trail miles north.

GREAT SMOKY MOUNTAINS NATIONAL PARK (Tennessee/North Carolina)

This trail follows the crest of the Smokies, often right on the North Carolina-Tennessee border. Highlights in the park include Clingmans Dome (the highest point on the Appalachian Trail, easily reachable by day hikers), and Charlies Bunion, a rocky promontory with big views. Camping permits are required.

ROAN HIGHLANDS (Tennessee)

Roan Mountain, elevation 6,286 feet, is one of the trail's highest points. The treeless summits here are called balds. The cause of the lack of forest cover is debated. The mountains here are not high enough for elevation to be the cause; other possibilities include Native American burning cycles,

grazing, and winds. The open summits offer fabulous views, and the rhododendron in early summer is one of the most spectacular floral displays in the world. Expect rugged hiking.

GRAYSON HIGHLANDS STATE PARK AND MOUNT ROGERS NATIONAL RECREATION AREA (Virginia)

Mount Rogers, at 5,728 feet, is the Virginia high point, and is accessible via a short spur trail from the Appalachian Trail. Wild ponies—well habituated to human presence—may visit you at your campsite.

McAFEE KNOB (Virginia)

One of the trail's most photogenic beauty spots, this outcropping in southern Virginia in the Roanoke region near the Blue Ridge Parkway is second to none. The jutting shelf of rock that hangs over the valley provides a setting for dramatic photos.

SHENANDOAH NATIONAL PARK (Virginia)

The AT in Shenandoah National Park is ideal for day hikers because the trail and the road cross each other at frequent intervals, making short hikes of varying lengths easy to organize. The park is especially lovely in autumn. Camping permits are required.

BEAR MOUNTAIN RIDGE (Connecticut/Massachusetts)

An easy two-hour drive from the New York metropolitan area, the section of trail from Salisbury, Connecticut, to Jug End in Massachusetts is an ideal weekend backpack trip. Several trailheads enable different day hikes as well. The heart of this hike is a rocky ridge walk over Bear Mountain, the Connecticut high point. Near the Massachusetts border, Sages Ravine is a famed beauty spot and campsite.

PRESIDENTIAL RANGE, WHITE MOUNTAINS (New Hampshire)

New Hampshire's White Mountains are as rugged as they come, and the Presidential Range is the crown jewel of the experience. Somewhat mediating the harsh terrain, a series of mountain huts managed by the Appalachian Mountain Club offer bunk rooms and meals, making the camping cushier for those willing to pay the price. (Reservations are usually required.) Otherwise, camping is permitted in designated areas only (reservations are recommended). This is tough, tough, tough terrain with potentially dangerous weather, but the 100-mile views (on a good day) are worth the effort. The AT goes over the New

Hampshire high point, Mount Washington, which is accessible by foot, car, and cog railway. Day hikers at the summit should have proper equipment, including rain gear, a hat, and an extra layer of clothing.

THE MAHOOSUCS
(New Hampshire/Maine)

If you liked the Whites, you'll love the Mahoosucs, which continue the rock scrambling through Mahoosuc Notch, the "hardest mile on the trail." Whatever your normal daily hiking mileage is, cut it in half when you make your plans for this stretch of trail.

MAINE WILDERNESS (Maine)

This is the grand run-up to Katahdin—and relatively easy, at least in comparison to what came before. The highlight is finding the perfect nightly campsite at ponds and lakes.

KATAHDIN (Maine)

Mighty Katahdin shocked Henry David Thoreau with a glimpse into the inhuman soul of a fierce, uncaring mountain. His resulting description tells of a nature that sternly chases man back to the flatlands where he belongs. Hikers who venture to take on the five-mile climb should be prepared for some scrambling, including using cables bolted into the rock. The view from the top is unmatched. Katahdin is accessible to day hikers.

Top: Hiker on Charlies Bunion, Great Smoky Mountains National Park; *Middle Left:* Southern terminus of the AT, Springer Mountain; *Middle Right:* Wild pony, Grayson Highlands, Mount Rogers National Recreation Area; *Bottom:* The AT heading down Mount Katahdin, Baxter State Park

THE PACIFIC CREST TRAIL

In 1938, photographer Ansel Adams published a limited-edition book called *Sierra Nevada: The John Muir Trail*. Photography had long played a role in the American wilderness movement. In the 1800s in Wisconsin, Henry Hamilton Bennett promoted and popularized the stunning gorges of the Wisconsin Dells with images that were revolutionary for their time. In California, Carleton Watkins's pictures of Yosemite Valley led to Yosemite's designation as a state park in 1864 (it became a national park in 1890). And William Henry Jackson's photographs influenced Congress's decision to designate Yellowstone as America's first national park in 1872. • Adams's *Sierra Nevada: The John Muir Trail* made the rounds from the National Park Service to the desk of the secretary of the interior and thence to the White House. Two years later, in 1940, Kings Canyon National Park, which includes a long section of the

John Muir Trail, became a reality. National Park Service Director Arno Cammerer wrote to Adams saying, "I realize that a silent but most effective voice in the campaign was your book . . . "

The High Sierra, Yosemite, Kings Canyon, Mount Lassen, Mount Shasta, Crater Lake, the Three Sisters Wilderness, Mount Hood, Mount Rainier, Glacier Peak: the places of the Pacific Crest Trail (PCT) are landscapes that speak for themselves, although they have had to rely on writers, photographers, and politicians to carry their voices to those who could protect them. The names of these advocates are hardly less famous: John Muir, Ansel Adams, and William O. Douglas were among the writers, photographers, activists, and politicians who joined and directed the cause of the American wilderness movement, and all of them are associated with the PCT.

In the words of Clinton Clarke, one of the trail's founders: "In few regions of the world—certainly nowhere else in the United States—are found such a varied and priceless collection of the sculptured masterpieces of Nature as adorn, strung like pearls, the mountain ranges of Washington, Oregon, and California. The Pacific Crest Trailway is the cord that binds this necklace; each gem encased in a permanent wilderness protected from all mechanization and commercialization."

THE SECOND TWIN

The Pacific Crest Trail is America's second national scenic trail. Although named together and equally with the Appalachian Trail as one of the first two trails designated by the National Trails System Act of 1968, the PCT is, like a second twin, forever designated as "the younger." The AT was conceived first, finished as a continuous route first, and had the first thru-hikers, the first trail celebrities, the first fully formed and functional trail organization. But as far as wilderness is concerned, the PCT is second to none.

As siblings so often are, America's first two national scenic trails are both distinctly different from and surprisingly similar to each other, and the similarities and differences are worth exploring for those seeking to understand them—or trying to choose which one to hike.

Like any self-respecting elder sibling, the Appalachian Trail is well established, financially successful, and basks in relative security. It lives in comfortable proximity to Washington, DC's halls of power, where fund-raising and land-management issues are decided. It is well represented in the media—in both books and documentaries. Located near the big eastern cities, the AT has more resources to draw from, namely, more—and more populous—trail clubs, more members, more volunteers, more donors, more guidebooks, more trail signs, more trail towns, more trail festivals, more money. That is, more of almost everything. Except for wildness and scope and sheer grand mile-after-mile jaw-dropping scenic beauty. Those are the purview of the PCT.

The enormous roadless High Sierra, the craggy, cranky drylands of Southern California, the volcanoes and glaciers of the Cascades, the endless lava fields of Oregon, the sky-devouring western redcedars of Washington: even if the PCT had the budget and the manpower of the AT, it couldn't tame this wildness, couldn't bring any of it down to human scope and scale. There is nothing gentle and comforting about the PCT. In the face of a high snow year in the High Sierra, no budget-line item for trail maintenance, no number of volunteers, can melt the cornice at Forester Pass or make the snow-fed streams crossable in early June.

The PCT isn't about community in the wilderness, or conquering the wilderness. It is about melding with the wilderness and sometimes submitting to it; it is about experiencing a primeval America where wilderness is not an illusion, but still an enormous reality. To walk for two weeks without seeing a road, a power line, a structure, or a cell tower is an experience modern humans must seek. They find it here.

And they find protection as well. Much of the PCT is located on public land, particularly national forests, with long stretches through pristine wilderness areas managed by both the Forest Service and the Park Service. The PCT eschews the auto-accessible giant grove in Sequoia National Park and heads instead for the far eastern Sierra backcountry, where only foot travel can take you. It avoids the regulated, roaded tent cities of Yosemite Valley, but tramps instead in the Tuolumne High Country to trails that lead south toward high passes and spiky peaks, many of them snow tipped, even in summer. The PCT is designated for foot and stock traffic only—humans, horses, llamas, and mules, but no bicycles or motorized vehicles. Within two or three hours of the coastal cities, hikers find the same solace Benton MacKaye imagined the AT would provide: wilderness as a healing force and an antidote to contemporary urbanization.

It's not all wilderness, of course. The sad clear-cut forests south of Washington's Interstate 90 at Snoqualmie Pass are hardly encased in permanent wilderness protection, nor are the ranchlands along the Mojave Desert of California. Even in wilderness areas themselves, overuse by recreational users is a common problem, especially in sections easily accessible from major highways and population centers.

But Clinton Clarke's extraordinary and ambitious vision has mostly been realized. Over its Mexico-to-Canada length, the PCT manages to link one world-class beauty spot to the next, and even the paths in between—those "connecting corridors"—often rival or surpass the most stunning highlights of any other trail in the country. Mile for mile—and that means nearly 2,700 of them—the PCT may boast the most protected pathway through the most spectacular scenery of any trail in the system. Or, indeed, the world.

THE EVEREST OF HIKING TRAILS

The PCT is sometimes referred to as the Everest of hiking trails. In point of fact, though, more people have stood atop Mount Everest than have thru-hiked the PCT.

It's an apples-to-oranges comparison of course: One mighty push through the jaws of the death zone versus a half-year slog. One 30,000-foot mountain versus some 315,000 feet of elevation gain and 315,000 feet of elevation loss to be climbed and descended over a period of five or six months. What they do have in common is daunting challenge, daily drama, and a spectacular mountain experience.

Trying to compare the PCT to its twin sibling, the AT, is only slightly easier. Far fewer hikers attempt the PCT every year. In recent years, the number of starting self-declared thru-hikers, according to the Pacific Crest Trail Association, is thought to range from 500 to 800, approximately 60 percent of whom finish. (These numbers are apt to change with the growing publicity about the Pacific Crest Trail, following Cheryl Strayed's best-selling memoir *Wild*, and the eponymous feature film starring Reese Witherspoon.) That the PCT has a higher percentage of finishers than the AT may be because of the greater experience most PCT hikers bring to the trail: many of them are AT graduates.

Thru-hikers they may be, but once AT hiking boots hit western soil, they are in for a very different path. For one thing, the PCT is not about finding

community in the wilderness. Communities do form both in trail towns and at a growing number of events that take place at parks and campgrounds near the trail. But the trail community on the PCT is markedly different than on its eastern counterpart. For one thing, it is dwarfed and fractured by wilderness. Though the vast majority of PCT hikers start at the same time and in the same direction—northbound from Campo, California, in late April—without shelters at frequent intervals to cluster hikers together, and with far fewer people spread out over far more space, hikers tend to scatter, their paths intersecting less often.

Still, AT veterans persist in trying to import the culture of community to the PCT, carrying with them traditions like "trail names," "trail angels," and "trail magic." But these human constructs seem to have only a flimsy presence on a trail whose mountains, wilderness, and length simply swallow them up. In this much smaller community, a solo hiker can easily stay solo for days, weeks, or even months—a situation that suits some hikers far better than others. Given the much larger number of hikers on the AT, this difference may be one of the most important considerations for hikers seeking a backcountry, as opposed to a social, experience.

Interestingly, there is one unexpected way in which the Pacific Crest Trail is much easier than the Appalachian Trail. Both the AT and PCT are entirely marked and easy to follow from end to end. (In contrast, many of the other, younger national scenic trails have at least some sections that are still unfinished or not yet well marked, or where trail segments are separated by long stretches of connecting roads.) The difference is that the PCT's footway is graded for horses (and in many cases was created by horse packers for stock use). It hardly ever exceeds 10 percent, which means that the maximum elevation gain in a mile is no more than about 526 feet. In contrast, on the AT, 10-percent grades are considered easy hiking, and grades of 20 percent—gaining more than 1,000 feet in a mile—are not uncommon. On the AT, hikers must frequently climb and scramble, pulling themselves up and down rocks and boulders using their hands as well as their feet. Unless a thru-hiker is scrambling on an ice slope in late spring, the PCT almost never requires a hiker to use his or her hands. As a result, hikers on the PCT can make much faster and more comfortable mileage than they can on the AT.

OPPOSITE: Equestrians along the PCT, Vasquez Rocks Natural Area Park, California

FOLLOWING SPREAD: Joshua tree, Mojave Desert, California (top left); a tarn along Bighorn Plateau, Sequoia National Park, California (middle left); the PCT heading north along Bighorn Plateau, Sequoia National Park, California (bottom left); the PCT coming up from Bubbs Creek, Sequoia National Park, California (right)

The difficulties of the Pacific Crest Trail are in its ecological extremes. Only one other trail—the Continental Divide Trail—confronts hikers with a similar range of environmental challenges over a similar length. (The Arizona Trail has a similar range, but its mileage is less than a third of the PCT's.) On the PCT, these challenges include everything from the Mojave Desert to arctic-alpine tundra to ice-covered passes to miles of snowfields to dangerous river crossings to rain forests to the possibility of early autumn snowstorms. And, unlike trails that pass through more populated parts of the country, the side trails that can lead out of the wilderness in case of insurmountable problems are few and far between. Many have challenges of their own.

The length of the PCT compounded with the short snow-free window in the High Sierra and in the North Cascades adds to the difficulty. Unlike the Appalachian Trail, much of which is hikeable year-round, and which can be hiked over a six- or seven-month snow-free period, the PCT has a five-month, or at most six-month, window for a trail that is about 500 miles longer. For thru-hikers, that means that the average hiking day is somewhere in the 18- to 20-mile range, depending on how many days you take off for breaks and resupplying.

Finally, the trail has one last challenge for the new generation of tablet-carrying digital nomads. When hikers stride forth onto the PCT, they step back in time to an analog world. While hikers on the AT can upload photos to Facebook at reassuringly frequent intervals, or sit in a lean-to and text or even talk with friends back home, PCT hikers are only intermittently so lucky, with long stretches where cell phones seek signals to no avail, and the bars remain stubbornly at zero. For some, the cutting of the digital umbilical cord is unexpected and uncomfortable.

For others, it creates a sense of glorious freedom. The lack of digital connection enables a different sort of bond with the wilderness to form. Unable to escape the loneliness of a solo long-distance hike by chatting with a loved one or by viewing Facebook likes for their backcountry bravado, hikers are forced to confront the wildness head on, with all its uncertainty and mercurial changes. Hiking the PCT harks back to a different era of travel—an era when traveling truly meant leaving home, not only in the physical sense but also in the emotional sense. Back in time, in the analog world, being unable to check in easily with

family and friends forced the traveler to engage more fully with his or her surroundings. Zero bars is an old-fashioned way to travel.

A PATH OF EXTREMES

The extreme environments on the Pacific Crest Trail affect which sections are hikeable when. This is a concern for both section hikers, who must choose where to hike in any given season, and thru-hikers, who must deal with the fact that some sections of the trail have a very short hikeable window, particularly the North Cascades of Washington and the High Sierra of California, whose eight high passes may hold ice well into summer, and where rivers swollen from the annual snowmelt may be dangerous to ford.

Most thru-hikers arrive at Kennedy Meadows, the gateway to the High Sierra, in June. The topic of conversation at every campsite is the same: "Has the snow melted yet? Can we get across the high passes?" Conversation is fueled by online snow reports and rumors and the knowledge of past history. Some years, the Sierra is snow-free by June; other years, not until August. The depth of the winter snowpack and the warmth of the spring sun are known meteorological facts; the day-to-day reality of what hikers will find a week or so into the future is, however, a mystery, and the trail keeps its secrets, unbothered by technology. The only way to really know what lies ahead is to put one foot in front of the other.

On the opposite end of the spectrum are the desert sections of Southern California and the Mojave just south of the Sierra, where water sources can start to dry before spring is over, and where summer heat can rise to 120 degrees Fahrenheit or more. Adding to the challenge is the geography: in Southern California, the trail must climb and descend over a series of high ranges, a bit like a horse jumping hurdles—down to the heat, up to the pines. Start too late in the season and the low-elevation temperatures will be unbearable and the springs will be dry. Start too early, and you are likely to be stopped by thigh-deep snowfields. In some years, both might happen, even in the same day.

Conditions can vary drastically from year to year. The winter snowpack may be more or less, spring snowmelt may have occurred at different rates in different places. The trail in the Lagunas, just a day's walk north of the Mexican border, might be snow covered, while temperatures in the plains below

OPPOSITE: Wanda Lake, Evolution Basin, Kings Canyon National Park, California (top); Rainbow Falls, Devils Postpile National Monument, California (bottom)

FOLLOWING SPREAD: Deer in Tuolumne Meadows, Yosemite National Park, California (left); LeConte Falls, Tuolumne River, Yosemite National Park, California (top right); Sonora Pass, California (middle right); Heather Lake, Desolation Wilderness, California (bottom right)

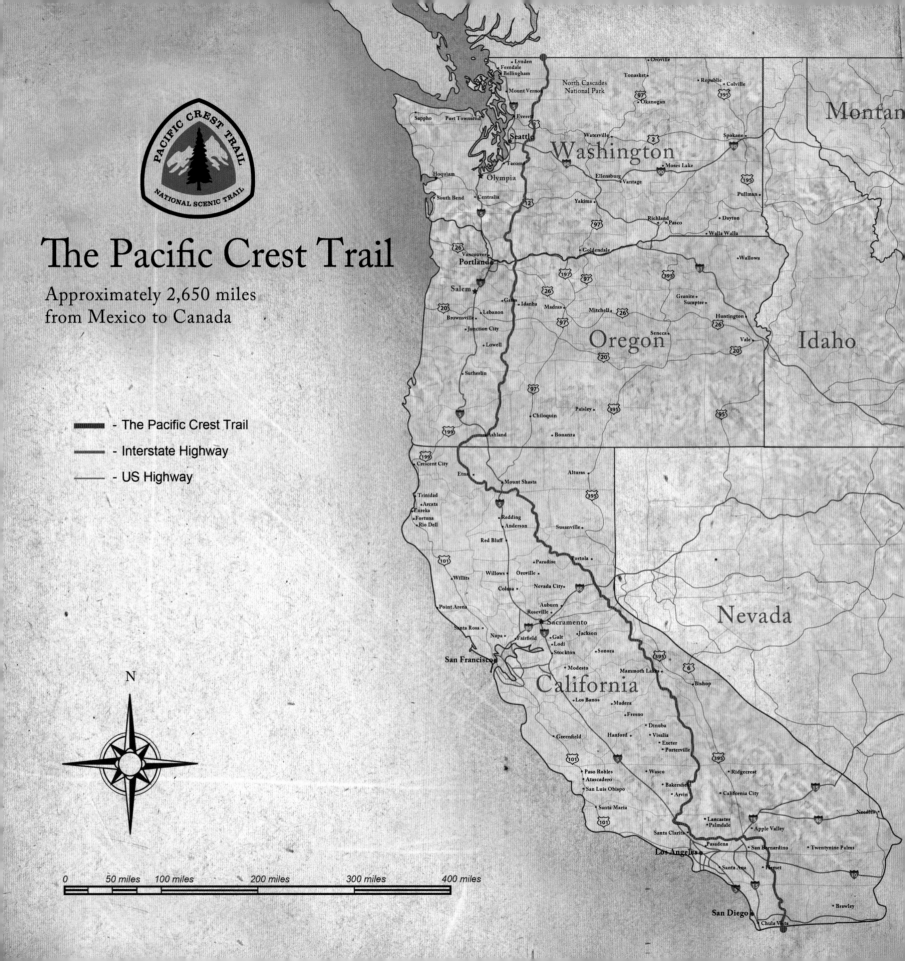

The Pacific Crest Trail

Approximately 2,650 miles
from Mexico to Canada

PACIFIC CREST TRAIL
NATIONAL SCENIC TRAIL

Legend

▬▬▬ - The Pacific Crest Trail
——— - Interstate Highway
——— - US Highway

N

0   50 miles   100 miles   200 miles   300 miles   400 miles

poke into the 90s. Typically, the snow-free window in the PCT's alpine sections extends from mid-June (for the hardiest hikers only) until sometime in late September or October, when winter comes again. The fact that the window for travel is so small means that thru-hikers tend to congregate at about the same starting date—sometime in late April. A now-traditional send-off party hosted by trail buffs and former thru-hikers at Lake Morena County Park focuses the start date even more.

Short-distance hikers, unencumbered by the Rubik's Cube of thru-hiking schedules, can have the best of all worlds, traveling as slowly as they like to savor scenery and experience, and tackling each section in its best season. Southern California might be better split into high and low sections, the high sections to be hiked as soon after snowmelt as possible (usually some time in May or June), and the low sections to be hiked earlier. The desert wildflower bloom in Anza-Borrego Desert State Park, which attracts nature lovers from around the world, usually takes place sometime in March. By contrast, July and August are the best months to tackle the High Sierra.

For thru-hikers and short-term hikers alike, the extreme environments found along the Pacific Crest Trail offer not only challenges, but also enormous natural wonders. The variety of landscapes ranges from low deserts to the highest peaks in the contiguous United States. The glaciated granite of the Sierra is different from the volcanic giants of the Cascades. The vegetation is as extreme as the terrain: Joshua trees, ancient bristlecone pines, towering Sequoias, and old-growth forests of stately Douglas firs and thousand-year-old western redcedars. The most extreme vegetation and wildlife is a product of the extreme environments to which they have adapted. Cacti hoard water in the south; in the high alpine meadows, wildflowers live an entire life cycle in a few short summer weeks; in the Pacific Northwest, the mosses, epiphytes, ferns, and giant conifers all soak in the shade-filtered sunlight and the endless water.

And hikers adapt too. It is one of the demands wilderness makes of them, one of the lessons it teaches: not to conquer but to coexist, not to fight, but to bend.

THE ROUTE

Going south to north (once again, following the preferred direction of thru-hikers), the Pacific Crest Trail begins in the arid borderlands of Southern California.

It's a tough start for unacclimated hikers. From the modest monument that marks the trail's southern terminus at the Mexican border, it is a 20-mile walk to the nearest perennial water source. And, to be perfectly honest, the desiccated landscape is not everyone's idea of a beauty spot. A bit farther into the hike, when their eyes get used to the variations of dusty browns and dull water-starved greens, hikers will start to see beauty in the wide brown vistas and the subtleties brought by changes in elevation. But at first, the PCT experience is all about acclimating to a harsh environment with too much sun, not enough water, and far too many shades of brown. Added to the startling uncomfortable newness of the experience are the back-of-the-mind warnings from guidebooks and from other hikers about encounters with the Border Patrol and Mexican immigrants crossing the border illegally. Crime is not unheard of. The safest option is a 20-mile first day to Lake Morena County Park. That's a rude awakening for bodies that are not yet trail hardened. Plus, there are rattlesnakes.

For the duration of Southern California—about the first 600 miles—northbound hikers walk against the grain of mountain formation. Hence, up and over, and up and over, and up and over again—the Lagunas, the San Jacintos, the San Gabriels, the Tehachapis (interspersed with a taste of the Mojave Desert, guarded by its signature Joshua trees)—and then, finally, the climb into the Sierra Nevada. The change in scenery is dramatic, from cacti up to shady pines, from baking hardpan dotted with creosote bushes to ancient wind-stunted Limber pines. In the approximately six weeks it takes most hikers to walk from the Mexican border to the southern edge of the High Sierra, bodies subtly, slowly acclimate to the lack of water, to walking all day, and to the sun and heat.

The next large section of the trail is the Sierra Nevada. From the Kennedy Meadows campground on the south end of the Sierra, hikers stride into 200 miles of wildlands that offer only a few inconvenient opportunities for off-trail resupply, no roads, and no cell-phone towers, not to mention those eight snow-clogged high passes. The trail here is contiguous with much of the 210-mile-long John Muir Trail. It is a world-class hiking destination and arguably one of the most beautiful places on the planet. It is also one of the big-ticket bucket-list hikes in North America. Even with a permit system, expect crowds in July and August.

PREVIOUS SPREAD: Banner Peak near Island Pass, Ansel Adams Wilderness, California

FOLLOWING SPREAD: The PCT along Golden Canyon, Carson-Iceberg Wilderness, California (left); Burney Falls, McArthur-Burney Falls Memorial State Park, California (right)

The "high" part of the High Sierra is generally understood as ending around Sonora Pass, at the north end of Yosemite National Park. From Sonora Pass north, hikers are in the plain old regular Sierra Nevada, where elevations are lower and the road crossings are more frequent, but the views are often just as spectacular, particularly in early summer, when the wildflowers bloom in alpine meadows. Like hikers, the flowers are on a mission to get all their business—in this case, a full life cycle from birth to reproduction to death—finished in the short snow-free window. Here, the landscape alternates between granite pinnacles reminiscent of the glory country to the south, and drier, volcanic formations with weirdly sculpted lava outcroppings. After the Desolation Wilderness, the trail will never again top 10,000 feet.

In Northern California, the character of the trail continues to soften, mellowing to lower, more forested mountains as the trail approaches the Cascades. Forests—and forestry—begin to dominate: some of the land is logged, parts are grazed, and the multiple-use mandate of the Forest Service is evident, as is the history of the region as the center of California's gold rush. With fewer population centers, the trail is less well maintained in some of the national forest stretches that might be thought of connectors between the "pearls" on Clinton Clarke's necklace.

Highlights of the trail here include Castle Crags State Park and Mounts Lassen and Shasta, the first of the Cascade volcanoes. Rather than continuing straight north, the trail in Northern California swings in a wide western arc, adding miles to the journey before the elusive Oregon border. The summers can be hot and dry here, and spirits can flag as long-distance hikers realize they have walked nearly 1,600 miles and have yet to cross a state border.

Finally, the PCT reaches its first state line, entering Oregon just south of Ashland. Now fully in the Cascades, the trail picks up momentum. The path itself is among the smoothest on any national scenic trail. If you're of the mindset to do so, it's possible to hike 30 or 35 miles a day here as you tick past volcanoes: Mount Thielsen (the "lightning rod of the Cascades," because the glassy fulgurite that caps its summit was created by lightning), Three-Fingered Jack (named for its spires), the Three Sisters of the Three Sisters Wilderness (and their attendant little brother and other family members, all surrounded by enormous lava fields), and then—growing more

impressive—Mount Washington, Mount Jefferson, and finally Oregon's high point, Mount Hood. Most hikers spend their last day in Oregon off the official route of the PCT, taking instead the popular Eagle Creek Trail to descend from the southern side of Mount Hood to the Columbia River.

Crossing the Columbia River on the Bridge of the Gods, the trail enters Washington and continues to tick off volcanoes: around the base of Mount Adams with the shattered remains of semi-decapitated Mount St. Helens to the west, a ridge walk through the Goat Rocks Wilderness, and then a run along the east side of Mount Rainier skirting the edge of its eponymous national park. North of Interstate 90, the trail heads into the popular Alpine Lakes Wilderness, hikes around the flanks of Glacier Peak, and makes its final push through the North Cascades to the Canadian border.

OPPOSITE: Howlock Mountain, Mount Thielsen Wilderness, Oregon

ABOVE: Mount Hood from Lolo Pass area, Oregon

FOLLOWING SPREAD: The PCT near Panther Creek, Gifford Pinchot National Forest, Washington (top left); Mount St. Helens from the PCT near the Sawtooth Berry Fields, Indian Heaven Wilderness, Washington (bottom left); the PCT heading north toward Mount Rainier, Goat Rocks Wilderness, Washington (right)

OPPOSITE: Catwalk along
the PCT, Alpine Lakes
Wilderness, Washington

RIGHT: Lake Valhalla and
Lichtenburg Mountain,
Henry M. Jackson
Wilderness, Washington

FOLLOWING SPREAD: Pika,
Glacier Peak Wilderness,
Washington (top left);
the PCT along Tamarack
Peak, Pasayten Wilderness,
Washington (middle left);
black bear, Glacier Peak
Wilderness, Washington
(bottom left); hikers on
the PCT ascending from
Canyon Creek, Pasayten
Wilderness (right)

THE PACIFIC CREST TRAIL

Mile for mile, the PCT may be the most jaw-dropping long trail in America. Even its connecting segments—the stretches between big mountains and scenically overloaded wildernesses areas—would be destinations in their own right on other trails. Some of the highlights below were chosen simply because they are among the best hikes anywhere in the world; some of them require several days or a week. Others were chosen for accessibility: to give day hikers and weekend hikers the chance to experience some of the trail's highlights. Accessibility means potential crowds, and many of these hikes require permits for overnight camping; some of the wilderness areas also require permits for day hiking (usually in self-service stations at the entry to the trails).

MOUNT BADEN-POWELL (California)

The high point of the San Gabriels can be reached by a day hike from the Angeles Crest Highway. One of the highlights of this hike is seeing the wind-stunted Limber pines along the crest; some Limber pines have been dated at more than 2,000 years old, making them among the oldest trees on earth. The PCT intersects the highway frequently on its run along the crest, making it possible to arrange day hikes and short backpack trips of varying lengths.

MOUNT WHITNEY (California)

California's 13,494-foot high point is not on the Pacific Crest Trail, but reaching its summit requires only a day hike off-trail. It's a detour most thru-hikers are happy to take the time to do. The summit can also be done in an overnight hike from the eastern (Lone Pine) side, but requires a hard-to-get permit.

THE JOHN MUIR TRAIL (California)

One of the absolute peak experiences of hiking anywhere in the world, the 210-mile-long John Muir Trail is contiguous with the Pacific Crest Trail for about 150 miles. Except for its start in Yosemite Valley (off the PCT), this trail is only accessible to backpackers. It includes the high passes of the High Sierra, with much of the route above 10,000 feet. Permits and bear canisters are required.

DESOLATION WILDERNESS (California)

North of the High Sierra near Lake Tahoe, this popular wilderness is a chance for day hikers and weekend hikers to experience terrain similar to that of the High Sierra: glacially formed alpine lakes, granite pinnacles, and classic Sierra high country. Permits are required.

CASTLE CRAGS STATE PARK (California)

A notable rock formation gives its name to the park, which ranges in elevations from 2,000 to 6,500 feet. Because of its location just off Interstate 5 between Castella and Dunsmuir, the park is popular with tourists of all stripes, but PCT hikers soon stride away from the crowds.

THREE SISTERS WILDERNESS (Oregon)

On the northern edge of the Three Sisters Wilderness, Old McKenzie Highway (Route 242) goes smack through the middle of enormous lava fields that cover the ground as far as the eye can see, ending only in snow-capped peaks. Easily accessible, this lava-strewn landscape makes for a fascinating day hike—or longer.

MOUNT HOOD (Oregon)

The PCT circles the west flank of Oregon's highest point at the 6,000-foot tree line. A special addition to starting a hike here is the possibility of staying at Timberline Lodge, meticulously crafted by Civilian Conservation Corps artisans in the 1930s in the "parkitecture style."

EAGLE CREEK TRAIL (Oregon)

Not officially on the Pacific Crest Trail, the famous and popular Eagle Creek Trail is taken by the majority of PCT hikers and is considered an "alternate" route, if not an official one. The trail passes scores of waterfalls as it descends to the Columbia River Gorge. Its north end is easily accessible by road. Easy treadway (at least along the creek; the climb from the creek to the trail is steep) and dozens of campsites make it ideal for both day hikers and weekenders.

GOAT ROCKS WILDERNESS (Washington)

With Highway 12 at White Pass on its northern end, this relatively small wilderness makes for an accessible weekend hike featuring a knife-edge ridge walk with exceptional views.

ALPINE LAKES WILDERNESS (Washington)

An accessible location just north of Interstate 90 makes the Alpine Lakes Wilderness an extremely popular destination. Named after its mountain lakes, the wilderness offers a stunning introduction to the PCT in Washington, with views back to Mount Rainier.

GLACIER PEAK WILDERNESS (Washington)

Less accessible to day hikers and weekenders, the Glacier Peak Wilderness in northern Washington is one of the PCT's top longer backpacking destinations. The boulder fields on the flanks of Glacier Peak are spectacular, with views straight up the craggy, glacier-scoured mountain. This is one of the places where the awe-inspiring power of both volcanoes and glaciers are displayed in all their raw grandeur.

STEHEKIN (Washington)

This fascinating and unique mountain community on Lake Chelan is not accessible by road from anywhere. To get there, you must walk, ride a horse, take a ferry, or fly in a floatplane across the lake. But Stehekin is the gateway to the PCT in this part of the remote North Cascades, and is a good place to start a backpacking trip south toward Glacier Peak.

Top: Glacier Peak, Glacier Peak Wilderness; *Middle Left:* John Muir Hut, Kings Canyon National Park; *Middle Right:* Timberline Lodge, Mount Hood; *Bottom:* Castle Crags State Park

THE CONTINENTAL DIVIDE TRAIL

➤ THE WILD CHILD ◄

What's in a name? Plenty, according to the traditions of Native Americans, including those who once lived—and in many cases still live—along the Continental Divide. According to the Navajo, names have power over the spirit; according to the Shoshone, a name can describe a person or encapsulate his or her most important qualities. Some naming ceremonies involve quests. A name is nothing to be given, or taken, lightly.

• The Continental Divide: it is perhaps the most audacious name of all the national scenic trails. Just think of it: something that divides a continent. What power it must have. • Stand on a high ridge of alpine tundra in Colorado. To the west is the Pacific watershed, and any rain that falls on that side of the Divide will end up in the Pacific Ocean (theoretically at least; in reality, it's more likely to disappear into the ground and go nowhere). But assuming for a whimsical moment that the little collection of raindrops finds a stream to join, and assuming the little stream doesn't first evaporate, or isn't siphoned into fountains in Las Vegas or sucked into an irrigation pump in California, then the raindrops would indeed flow to, or at least toward, the Pacific Ocean. Rain born in the same clouds, but that falls just a few inches to the east, will head on an even longer journey east to the Atlantic Ocean via the Gulf of Mexico (the same caveats apply). As if that isn't enough, there's also a spot up north in Montana where a secondary divide sends water to the Arctic Ocean.

Need proof? Seeing is believing, and you can even watch the Continental Divide as it goes about its business. In Wyoming's Bridger-Teton Wilderness, Two Ocean Creek rushes down the Divide, and at a spot called Parting of the Waters, the creek divides in half. Waters that formerly ran together separate to flow to destinations more than 3,000 miles apart.

Mention of the Continental Divide in the written historical record goes back to the earliest explorers who came this way, even in desiccated New Mexico, where the division of water is theoretical more than practical. The earliest white explorers were Spaniards, more concerned with travel between central Mexico and the Rio Grande, but their records indicate recognition of the existence of a great watershed divide. And knowledge of the Divide goes back much farther than that. Not only has the idea of a continental divide been a steadfast concept in the recorded history of the West at least since the 18th century; before that, it was a steadfast reality to the Native Americans who lived here first.

So it seems strange, sometimes, to a hiker, that this divide, so mighty in myth—history stopping, continent splitting—is not always as obvious as all that. It may loom large in imagination and history, but on the ground, the Continental Divide is not the monolithic barrier one might imagine. It is not some natural Great Wall of China striding up and down the landscape linking the highest points of the mountain west.

In point of fact, watershed divides don't work that way. Instead, they may simply comprise a series of different discrete ridges that lie on the land in such a way that they all funnel their waters the same way. More than just a high point decides the flow of water: topography, slant, grade, outlets, and drainage all play a role, too. While it's always obvious which way the water might fall on any given slope, it's not always obvious where it might end up as it twists and turns

from rivulet to brook to stream to river; as it carves and finds paths in the undulating lands below.

Seen from ground level by a hiker standing on one ridge among many, the Continental Divide doesn't wear a sign: it is just one of many heights of land, one of many ridges, all of which jumble themselves together to create a sea of mountains. With tricks of light and the differing perspectives of distance and elevation, finding the Divide is often far less obvious than one might expect. For a hiker standing on a ridge in a fog, it is sometimes impossible to see. Yet the Divide remains not only a massive idea, but also a force that history finds impossible to ignore.

It's also a landscape that hikers find impossible to ignore: wild and remote, above tree line for miles at a time, it is an obvious magnet for long-distance hikers. It is not, however, always easy for trail builders. Although great progress has been made to complete the Continental Divide Trail (CDT) since it was authorized in 1978, some of it remains in the planning stages, and much of it is only infrequently marked. Where the trail is not yet designated, CDT hikers often "make" their own route, following the suggestions of those who have gone before or improvising their own paths through trailless wildlands. It sometimes seems possible, standing alone in a hidden New Mexico arroyo, to think that no one else has ever stumbled into this particular box canyon, let alone found a way out of it. Or, bashing through the thickets of a Montana forest, where the trail has petered out into nothing more than a game path, you might ask the question—"Could I possibly be the first to set foot just exactly here?"

And that's when you might see the wheel ruts of the wagons of the Oregon Trail, or an old mine shaft, or the remains of a well long abandoned. Even in a forgotten box canyon in the middle of no place anyone would ever go if they were looking for safety and comfort, the traces of those who went before are deeply etched on the land.

So it's only a pretty hiker conceit—fed by the grand isolation of the Continental Divide, looking out over so much ice and rock and open empty space—that you are walking over land untouched by human footsteps. The truth could not be more different. Quite simply, the Continental Divide has been a barrier to every movement west, from the earliest Native American traders to the fur trappers and mountain explorers to the emigrant trains to the gold miners

and railroads. One can only imagine the reaction of settlers racing across the flat lands of Kansas and eastern Colorado when they suddenly saw the mountain wall ahead. Miners, settlers, cattlemen, criminals: all tried to cross, and all left behind their debris—cabins, tools, mines, holes, windmills now broken and flailing in the breeze. This wild place, this most untamed of all the national scenic trails, is also a 3,100-mile-long outdoor museum of American history.

True, other national scenic trails commemorate history as well. The Potomac Heritage Trail and the Natchez Trace Trail, for example, along with parts of the New England Trail and the North Country Trail, bear marks of a gentler passage of humans across the land, and, sometimes, the violent marks of human encounters with each other. What is different on the CDT is that here an isolated and wild landscape is dotted with the detritus of the battle between man and mountain, the remains of the quest to cross this divide. Crumbling settlements, lonely shacks on empty land,

old roads and paths, old military stations founded to protect settlers and emigrants from threats long since vanished: all of these tell stories of human migration and settlement and hope. And the graves, marked and unmarked, on the Oregon Trail—the graves tell the stories of despair. The Divide is a place where men wrestled with mountains and did not always win.

THE WILD CHILD

Perhaps the only thing as audacious as the idea of a continent-splitting, history-stopping watershed is the prospect of creating a trail that follows its crest. The Continental Divide Trail owes much of its existence to the work of one man, Jim Wolf, who has spent decades plotting out possible hiking routes, writing guidebooks, and lobbying the United States Forest Service on issues pertaining to the trail's routing as a minimum-impact path (in the words of Wolf, a "silent" trail). Wolf's Continental Divide Trail Society (CDTS) supports hikers with maps, information, and on-the-ground observations. Also working on the trail—raising money, coordinating volunteers, and giving input into routing and usage decisions—have been the now-defunct nonprofit Continental Divide Trail Alliance, which functioned from 1995 to 2011, and the new Continental Divide Trail Coalition. The Forest Service is the lead agency on the government side.

Since its designation as the nation's third national scenic trail in 1978, enormous strides have been made in developing the CDT and finalizing its route. However, the combination of a fierce landscape, a complex patchwork of landownership, and local suspicion of federal government projects is a recipe for slow progress. Conflicting uses—logging, grazing, mining, energy and water projects (including wind turbines and transmission lines), development of residential areas, and recreational use ranging from whisper-in-the-wilderness no-trace cross-country skiers to mountain bikers to roaring ATVs and snowmobiles to downhill ski areas to packs of Boy Scouts—throw up a complicated tangle of issues that must be resolved before a trail can be designated. Nature doesn't always cooperate, either. Fires, floods, and mudslides have all taken out sections of completed trail, which must then be relocated or rebuilt—and the process begins all over again. In the meantime, the CDTS remains a trustworthy source of information regarding the current status of routes that are on the ground and ready to be hiked.

BELOW: The CDT through San Pedro Parks Wilderness, New Mexico

OPPOSITE: The Rio Chama along Chama Canyon, Santa Fe National Forest, New Mexico

Its website directs hikers to current sources for maps and other trail information.

So the landscape is extreme and the notion of creating a trail along it audacious; what then is to be said of the few people each year who attempt to actually hike the whole thing? By some estimates, more than 3,000 people have climbed Mount Everest. More than 10,500 athletes competed in the London Olympics. More than 500 people have gone into space. But estimates of the number of CDT finishers are only somewhere in the very low hundreds.

This hike is difficult, in all the usual ways, and then some. First of all, there is the length, which is a matter of some debate because the trail is not yet complete. As a result, hikers have a choice of routes—often some combination of preexisting trail, dirt roads, paved roads, or cross-country travel—to link together existing stretches of marked designated trail, particularly in New Mexico, but also in parts of Wyoming and along the Idaho-Montana border. The proposed route corridor approved in the National Trails System Act is 3,100 miles long. Most current hikers figure a route around 2,700 miles; some of the difference is due to routing shortcuts or to unfinished stretches of trail where road walks, which are often more direct than trails, are used.

As with the Pacific Crest Trail, much of the difficulty of hiking the CDT in one year revolves around the alignment of miles and mountains. No matter what direction of travel—south to north or north to south—the trail offers five months of reasonably certain snow-free hiking time; any longer and dangerous snowfields in late spring or early storms in autumn can block the path. In spring, snow conditions in Colorado's South San Juans and Montana's Glacier National Park can be dangerous. In the fall, northbounders don't want to risk being trapped in the big, high lonesome of Montana's Bob Marshall Wilderness, and southbounders face the same issue in Colorado's South San Juans, when the first snows roll in by October. Assuming a round-number 3,000-mile route and a five-month hike, the numbers work out to 20 miles a day, day in day out, with no days off. On a 2,700-mile route, the daily average drops to 18 miles a day. But in both cases, the actual mileage of an average hiking day will be quite a bit higher, because of time lost to resupplying in towns that may be 30 miles from the trail. Finding a ride to town, doing laundry, grabbing a shower, buying supplies, getting broken gear fixed, picking up packages at the post office, repacking, and hitching back again can easily take a full day or even two, and the mileage lost to rest and errands must be made up because winter is coming, winter is coming, winter is coming.

It doesn't help that some of the miles are slow. Without a fully marked trail, navigation remains a challenge on the Continental Divide Trail. Sometimes segments of trail are completed, but the finished section may end in the middle of nowhere, leaving the hiker to piece together bits of existing unmarked trails and roads—or to go cross country. Where trails do exist, they may be marked inconsistently or sometimes not at all.

Terrain adds to the challenge: In New Mexico, long stretches with little water force high-mileage days. In Colorado, the trail stays above 11,000 feet for almost the entire state, with lung-busting climbs to exposed ridges where afternoon thunderstorms add drama and sometimes terror. In southern Wyoming, hikers who choose the original CDTS guidebook route follow the trail, and, near the Sweetwater River and the Oregon Trail, cross the Divide at windswept South Pass, which lies between Wyoming's desolate Great Divide Basin (the so-called Red Desert) to the south and the fierce Wind River Mountains to the north. In Montana and Idaho, hikers might be forewarned by Lewis and Clark, who described a path "over rocky hill Sides where our horses were in pitial danger of Slipping to Ther certain distruction & up & Down Steep hills, where Several horses fell. Some turned over, and others Slipped down Steep hill Sides [sic]." The CDT does not take the same path that gave Lewis and Clark's horses so much trouble, but the region remains very much the same: the explorers would recognize those same steep hillsides just south of Lost Trail Pass, reputedly named after some of their difficulties here.

So, to return to the Triple Crown family of trails: there is the Appalachian Trail, the staid eldest child, all grown up, confident in its ways, well funded and well connected. The AT knows the rules of the game and plays it well, successfully lobbying for money and protection from Capitol Hill, and building a network of supporting communities and passionate patrons. The Pacific Crest Trail, in true second-child fashion, alternates between emulating its sibling and forging its own path: it doesn't have a museum, or a land trust, or conferences that attract hundreds of members, but it gets the job done.

The Continental Divide Trail is the wild child, the unpredictable youngest; everything about it is iconoclastic, unpredictable, mercurial, quixotic. The Continental Divide Trail Society stays resolutely outside the orbit of the Forest Service bureaucracy, seeking only to represent its and its members' interests in a silent minimum-impact trail that follows a route offering the best primitive recreation values— wildness, protection, a good footpath, scenery, and access to the actual Divide when possible—regardless of whether such a route is politically feasible or even seen as possible. The new Continental Divide Trail Coalition is starting to find its feet and is working steadily toward the goal of uniting a disparate and far-flung group of trail supporters.

Part of the CDT's problem—and part of its glory— is its lack of a dense population base. The Appalachian and Pacific Crest Trails parallel the populous coastal regions of the United States, from which they can draw supporters, volunteers, donors, and advocates. By contrast, the only population centers reasonably near the CDT are Denver, Colorado, and Albuquerque, New Mexico. What the CDT feeds, therefore, is hikers' wildest dreams. Except in the national parks, it is entirely possible to hike hundreds of miles of the CDT and see no one—not another hiker—for weeks on end. There are more miles than volunteers, and it may be years before trailblazers get to a particularly gnarly remote section of trail. Such are the trade-offs of the Wild Child.

THE ROUTE

Let's get one thing straight—or as straight as possible when discussing a winding, climbing 3,100-mile mountain path that zigs and zags over peaks and valleys. The Continental Divide Trail follows the actual Divide only loosely. (The directives established when the CDT was designated a national scenic trail offer a wide margin, requiring only that the trail be within 50 miles on either side of the Divide.) Simply, it is not possible for a hiker to walk on the crest of the watershed all the way from Mexico to Canada.

Sometimes the impossibility is physical: rocks, ice, cliffs that plunge a vertical several hundred feet, climbs that would make a mountain goat quake on its hooves. And sometimes the impossibility is human: someone owns the land and says no. Through all this, the trail does try to run as close as possible to the Divide, but as far away as necessary to provide for safe

travel and diverse recreation appeal, to be economically feasible, and to keep environmental impacts to an acceptable level. Balancing all of this is not easy, but the official route does attempt to run as close as practical to the Divide.

Approximately 70 percent of the trail is complete; most of the remaining 30 percent is currently on dirt roads, undesignated and unmarked trails, or, rarely, requires walking on paved roads. In some sections, cross-country travel may be a more efficient option. Most of the finished miles are in national parks and national forests, as well as some Bureau of Land Management (BLM) lands. As a rule, lands managed for wilderness have particularly good trail tread (although marking trails in wilderness areas is controversial and often minimal). But on state land, BLM-administered land, and nonwilderness Forest Service land, the trail is only one of many competing interests, and hikers must often follow old dirt roads or stride out cross country, armed with maps, compasses, and a GPS. In the rare instance where the trail crosses private property, hikers must hope that any landowners encountered en route will continue to give their permission to pass through.

Adding to the confusion about trail routing is the fact that the route recommended by (and described in the guidebooks of) the private sector Continental Divide Trail Society is not always the route chosen by the Forest Service to be the official CDT footway. The Forest Service's decisions must take into account landownership and preexisting usage. While the CDTS usually follows the official route, there are places where the two entities differ in opinion on how best to route the trail when it can't run right along the Divide. Hikers have to make choices—and plan their map acquisitions, route selection, and resupplies—accordingly.

This is most evident at the southern terminus and the first third of New Mexico. The CDT starts on the Mexican border, but where? The official trail marker is located at Crazy Cook Monument, a remote marker in the boot heel, difficult to access even with a pickup, although recently, the BLM has granted a license for a hiker shuttle to operate during the spring and fall thru-hiking seasons. The CDTS guidebooks recommend a start at the border station in Columbus, New Mexico, a good 50 miles to the east but still within the official 50-mile corridor. The CDTS route takes hikers through areas of historic interest such

FOLLOWING SPREAD: The CDT along Knife Edge, Weminuche Wilderness, Colorado (top left); a camp below the Window, Weminuche Wilderness, Colorado (bottom left); the CDT through Weminuche Wilderness, Colorado (right)

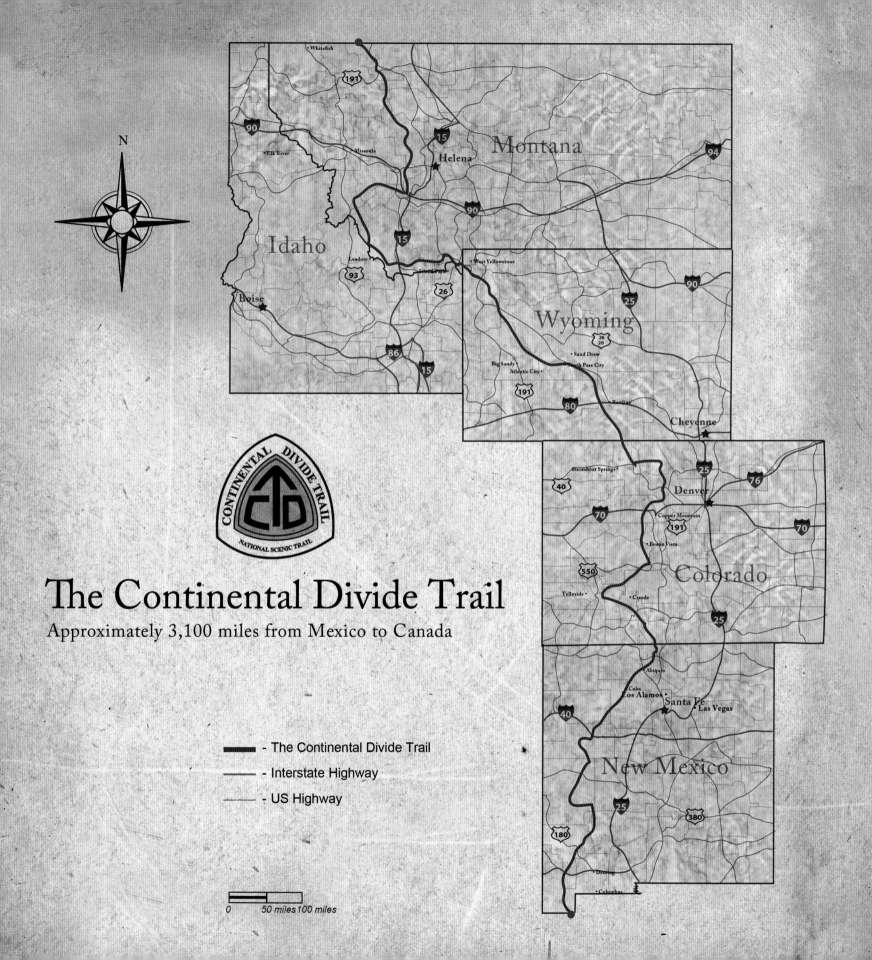

The Continental Divide Trail

Approximately 3,100 miles from Mexico to Canada

- **━━━** - The Continental Divide Trail
- ─── - Interstate Highway
- ─── - US Highway

0   50 miles 100 miles

as old Fort Cummings (near well-named Massacre Peak), the Cookes Spring Station on the Butterfield stage route, and the famed Gila Cliff Dwellings National Monument. The official route and the guidebook route continue to diverge through much of southern New Mexico, although most of the major resupply towns—Reserve, Pie Town, Grants, Cuba, and Chama—are the same.

The general route of travel through New Mexico links together the Gila, Cibola, Santa Fe, and Carson National Forests. In between—on state land, BLM land, private land, and Native American land—some of the route is still undetermined. As new decisions are made regarding possible routings, relocations of already existing trail may sometimes become necessary to make all the ends line up.

North of Interstate 40, the trail heads over Mount Taylor (the CDTS route goes over the summit, while the official route goes around its flanks). The route from Grants to Cumbres Pass near the Colorado border takes a line from southwest to northeast, with both the CDTS route and the official route passing through Cuba, north of Abiquiu, and up to Cumbres Pass.

In Colorado, the guidebook route and the official route are more or less in agreement. Starting at Cumbres Pass, the trail heads up to the South San Juans, "up" being the operative word: the CDT in Colorado has an average elevation well above 10,000 feet. The mountain ranges line up, each one offering more scenery than the last. In the San Juans, the trail through the Weminuche Wilderness heads west to loop around the headwaters of the Rio Grande; near the river's source, the CDT joins with the Colorado Trail. In the Cochetopa Hills, the CDT continues to follow the route of the Colorado Trail, with which it is mostly contiguous for about 200 miles until central Colorado. Through the Sawatch Range, the trail avoids the exposed high country except for a few above-tree-line segments. Just north of the ski town of Copper Mountain, it makes up for it with a newly constructed spectacular high-country stretch, while an alternate farther from the Divide affords an option that avoids the mountain crests and is mostly out of reach of lightning bolts from the daily afternoon storms. Finally, in northern Colorado, the trail skirts Rocky Mountain National Park and passes close to Steamboat Springs before exiting the state via a traverse of the Mount Zirkel Wilderness.

The trail in Wyoming is a bit of a cross between the CDT in New Mexico and in Colorado, with Yellowstone National Park thrown in to make things interesting. The CDT enters Wyoming in the Medicine Bow-Routt National Forest, and descends to Rawlins, on the southern side of the Great Divide Basin. The basin is a unique feature on the Continental Divide, which splits here into two arcs that form a circle. Water that falls inside that circle has outlets to neither the Atlantic Ocean nor the Pacific, but simply drains into the thirsty ground of the so-called Red Desert. At the northern end of the basin, South Pass City marks the place where emigrant trains, Pony Express postal riders, and Mormon pioneers crossed the Divide on the Oregon Trail.

Then it's back up to the high country, to the Wind River Mountains of the Bridger-Teton Wilderness, where the trail follows a spectacularly scenic route at elevations of 10,000 feet, just beneath the jutting pinnacles of the Divide and along the Green River. Between the Wind River Mountains and Yellowstone, the CDT continues through the Bridger-Teton National Forest, sometimes on multiple-use lands, and sometimes in wilderness, until it reaches the park boundary deep in the backcountry on the southern edge of the park. In Yellowstone, the trail follows the Snake River for a bit, lingers at a series of lakes, passes backcountry geyser basins, and then pokes into the front country around Old Faithful. To leave the park, it cuts west through the fire-scarred Madison Plateau and enters Idaho just before the park's western border.

The Continental Divide forms a crooked, meandering border between southern Idaho and southern Montana. The route generally stays close to the Divide, following the state border through a series of ridges, forests, open uplands, and peaks to Chief Joseph Pass in the Bitterroots, where the Divide swings east and the border continues straight north. From here north, the CDT is solely in Montana, starting with the lake-dotted and mountain-framed Anaconda-Pintler Wilderness. In mid-Montana, the trail becomes a bit of a hodgepodge, mostly on non-motorized trail, but some sections are located on dirt roads or multiple-use trails as well. The state saves its best for last in a triple-threat display: the enormous wilderness complex of the Scapegoat Wilderness, the Bob Marshall Wilderness, and, finally, Glacier National Park.

PREVIOUS SPREAD: View of Peru Creek Valley from the CDT, Arapaho National Forest, Colorado (left); mountain goats, Arapaho National Forest, Colorado (top right); prayer flags, Mount Edwards, Arapaho National Forest, Colorado (middle right); bull moose, Junco Lake, Arapaho National Forest, Colorado (bottom right)

OPPOSITE: The CDT entering an aspen grove, Cochetopa Hills, Gunnison National Forest, Colorado

FOLLOWING SPREAD: The CDT along Stanley Mountain, Arapaho National Forest, Colorado (left); Sheep Mountain, along a road section of the CDT near Rawlins, Wyoming (right)

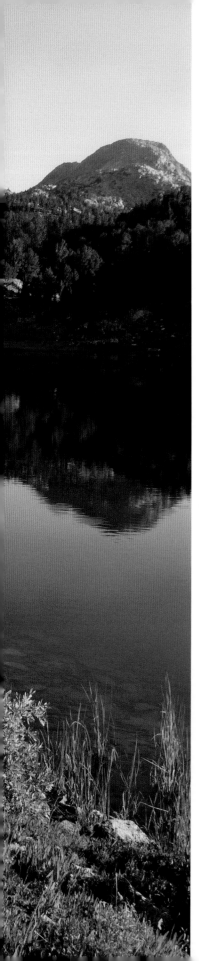

PREVIOUS SPREAD: Artemisia Geyser, Upper Geyser Basin, Yellowstone National Park, Wyoming (left); lodgepole pines on the shore of Summit Lake, Yellowstone National Park, Wyoming (right)

OPPOSITE: North Fork Peak along the Fremont Trail section of the CDT, Bridger-Teton National Forest, Wyoming

RIGHT: The CDT, Great Divide Basin, Wyoming (top); Coyote Gulch area, Great Divide Basin, Wyoming (middle); Crooks Mountain, Great Divide Basin, Wyoming (bottom)

FOLLOWING SPREAD: Rocks designating crossing of the CDT from Wyoming to Idaho, Yellowstone National Park, Wyoming (top left); pika, Hirschy Mountain, Beaverhead-Deerlodge National Forest, Montana (middle left); heart-shaped stone near the shore of Warren Lake, Anaconda-Pintler Wilderness, Montana (bottom left); the CDT near Morrison Lake, Beaverhead-Deerlodge National Forest, Montana (right)

PREVIOUS SPREAD: Warren Peak from across Warren Lake, Anaconda-Pintler Wilderness, Montana

LEFT: The CDT along Thunderbolt Mountain, Beaverhead-Deerlodge National Forest, Montana (top); the CDT through blooming fireweed along Strawberry Creek, Bob Marshall Wilderness, Montana (bottom)

OPPOSITE: Gates Park, Bob Marshall Wilderness, Montana

FOLLOWING SPREAD: Red Eagle Lake, Glacier National Park, Montana (left); Appekunny Falls, Glacier National Park, Montana (right)

THE CONTINENTAL DIVIDE TRAIL

The CDT has far too many highlights and beauty spots to cover in one short list, but the following picks, chosen for variety, give access to both day hikers and backpackers on shorter trips, as well as long-distance hikers. Some of these routes are on the official CDT route, some are on the CDTS guidebook route, and some are on both.

GILA WILDERNESS (New Mexico)

The CDTS's recommended route along the Gila River is much farther from the Divide than the approved, official route. But the river's beauty (not to mention the luxury of hiking along water) and the historic cliff dwellings are a welcome counterpoint to the drier sections to both the north and south. You'll cross the river about 100 times.

SAN PEDRO PARKS WILDERNESS (New Mexico)

One of the greenest sections of the CDT in New Mexico, the San Pedro Parks Wilderness is actually considered a southern finger of the Rocky Mountains and, fittingly, features a high plateau above 10,000 feet with well-marked trails and plenty of water.

GHOST RANCH (New Mexico)

In stark contrast to the green parks of San Pedro are the red rocks of Abiquiu. Georgia O'Keeffe painted the colorful buttes and bleached bones of northern New Mexico here. The red-rock country is stunning in both color and rock formations. Day hikes from Ghost Ranch are a good way to get a feel for this part of the trail.

WEMINUCHE WILDERNESS (Colorado)

In the San Juan Mountains, the CDT makes a wide western arc around the headwaters of the Rio Grande, staying largely on the crest of the Weminuche Wilderness. A multiday backpack trip, often along the crest of the Continental Divide, takes hikers into remote backcountry. If you have a four-wheel-drive vehicle, you can drive into the headwaters of the Rio Grande and strike out on spectacular day hikes from there.

MOUNT ELBERT (Colorado)

Colorado's high point near Twin Lakes is not on the Continental Divide, but it is a quick side trip from the Continental Divide Trail. It is easily accessible to day hikers, and with its endless views over Mount Massive and the Arkansas River Valley, it is a worthwhile detour for CDT long-distance hikers.

FRONT RANGE (Colorado)

The guidebook route traverses the actual ridge of the Continental Divide, going over five 13,000-foot peaks in a single day. In between those peaks, it scrambles up and down enormous, steep slopes of talus. Don't attempt this in bad weather: there is no cover, and the ridge is a virtual lightning rod. But this rugged traverse is the definition of a Rocky Mountain high. James Peak is accessible to day hikers via side trails.

MOUNT ZIRKEL WILDERNESS (Colorado)

In northern Colorado, the Mount Zirkel Wilderness is a bit less extreme than the terrain to the south. For backpackers seeking a somewhat gentler and very remote experience, it offers an alpine experience within range of protective tree cover.

SOUTH PASS (Wyoming)

The historic crossing of the Oregon Trail, the Mormon Battalion, and the Pony Express gives hikers the figurative experience of hiking in the footsteps of history. An interpretive center at South Pass City includes historic displays and demonstrations.

WIND RIVER RANGE (Wyoming)

An 80-mile stretch of the CDT runs from Big Sandy Opening to the Green River Lakes trailhead. This section of trail is largely above 10,000 feet, but involves mostly gentle grades, and well-marked (or, at least, easily followed) trail. Hikers more concerned with spectacular scenery than with making mileage and time might take alternate routes into the Cirque of the Towers and Titcomb Basin. Both detours require some climbing and scrambling.

YELLOWSTONE NATIONAL PARK
(Wyoming)

The trail passes Heart Lake, Shoshone Lake, and the Snake River, and makes a stop at Old Faithful. There are scores of day hikes within the park; for backpacking, permits are required. Wildlife sightings are an exciting bonus, but care must be taken to follow food-storage rules: this is grizzly country.

ANACONDA-PINTLER WILDERNESS
(Montana)

This pretty and—for Montana—smallish wilderness is a combination of jewel-like lakes set in alpine frames. It makes for an excellent short backpack trip, but day hikers can also find plenty of scenery within a few miles of their cars.

BOB MARSHALL WILDERNESS
CHINESE WALL (Montana)

This is the most popular hiking destination in the Bob Marshall Wilderness, the fifth-largest wilderness in the contiguous 48 states. The 1,000-foot escarpment runs along the Divide looking like a god-made Chinese Wall. A multiday backpack trip is required.

GLACIER NATIONAL PARK (Montana)

One of the crown jewels of the American National Park System, Glacier National Park is managed for wilderness values, and is home to one of the largest populations of grizzly bears in the contiguous 48 states. The route through the park includes a stop at Triple Divide Peak, which sends water three ways—to the Atlantic, Pacific, and Arctic Oceans. Permits are required.

Top: Old Faithful Geyser, Yellowstone National Park; *Middle Left:* Chimney Rock, Ghost Ranch; *Middle Right:* Gila Cliff Dwellings National Monument; *Bottom:* Chinese Wall, Bob Marshall Wilderness

THE NORTH COUNTRY TRAIL

Of all the national scenic trails, the North Country Trail (NCT) wins the prize for being the most difficult to define. Perhaps this is because of its length: at 4,600 miles, the nation's longest national scenic trail takes in landscapes ranging from the canals and vineyards of upstate New York to the tallgrass prairies of North Dakota where bison once thundered to infinite horizons, from the shores of Lakes Michigan and Superior to the small towns of Ohio and northern Wisconsin. Or perhaps it is because this is not a trail that simply follows easy-to-define geographic, geopolitical, or historic corridors—such as mountain ranges or historic routes of travel—but rather takes in an entire megaregion of the United States, resulting in unparalleled diversity. • This diversity makes it difficult to characterize the trail. Unlike most of the other national scenic trails, the

NCT—running from eastern New York through the upper Midwest to North Dakota—has no simple identity, no one photograph that springs to mind saying, "*This* is the North Country Trail." There are of course commonalities—a sort of L.L. Bean aesthetic, an understanding of what it is to live in a place where the heat is on six or seven months a year and snowblowers, snowplows, and snow skis are just a way of life. But this is a trail that transcends easy definition; it defies being neatly labeled and put into a box.

The North Country Trail Association (NCTA) characterizes the communities of the trail as being part of a "red plaid nation"—a sort of symbol that unites the diverse and varied northern places with the rugged peoples, past and present, who have managed to survive here and make it their home. It is the scratchy, rugged, durable emblem of the people drawn to the great north woods for fun, adventure, recreation, and spiritual reconnecting with the land along a sprawling footpath that links New York, the upper Midwest, and North Dakota—running from one of the most urban, populous, and liberal states in the nation to one of the most rural, least populated, and most conservative states.

So what is it that unites the wearer of a red plaid shirt in North Dakota with someone else in New York State—or southeastern Ohio? In many parts of the North Country Trail, it might be the shared experience of making a living in a harsh north-country environment. But even that experience extends beyond the borders of this trail, to New England, Canada, and the Pacific Northwest. Perhaps the real answer is that there is no answer. A valid argument could be made that, of all the national scenic trails, this is the one that best celebrates the diversity of small-town American life, perhaps offering the most complete look at the complexity of rural America—even while it eschews the extremes of high peaks, deserts, subtropics, and coasts. Perhaps the answer is that this trail is not a single thread, but a three-dimensional patchwork of towns, environments, communities, and ecosystems sewn together, perhaps by woolen threads of red and black.

WALKING THE AMERICAN NORTHLAND

The North Country Trail has not attracted nearly as many thru-hikers as the Appalachian Trail—nor even the Pacific Crest Trail or the Continental Divide Trail. For one thing, its 4,600-mile length makes the NCT by far the longest in the National Scenic Trails System. At 20 miles a day with no days off, it would take more than seven months to hike it; a more reasonable time frame would be eight or nine months. Long-distance hikers are used to big numbers—but perhaps not quite this big. And an eight- or nine-month hike through the North Country would involve the challenge of snow travel, something most long-distance hikers try to avoid.

Another issue that affects the choice of long-distance hikers is that while about 2,700 miles of the North Country Trail are currently complete—i.e., off of roads, on marked hiking footpaths—nearly 1,900 miles are on designated connector routes, many of them paved roads. So while the route as a whole is hikeable, prospective thru-hikers who prefer backcountry wilderness trails to roads are more likely to choose one of the trails with more finished backcountry footway and fewer miles of road walking.

And then there is simple habit: long-distance hikers tend to seek dramatic mountainscapes, and they almost always begin with the Appalachian Trail. Relatively few thru-hikers go on to hike a second megatrail, and if they do, they often choose the Pacific Crest Trail or the Continental Divide Trail.

Of course, long-distance hikers are a minority on any long-distance trail, and the National Trails System was not developed with thru-hiker needs in mind. To the contrary: one of the considerations in authorizing a national scenic trail is evaluating how its recreational resources serve the larger community. Within a day's drive of 40 percent of the population of the United States, the North Country Trail offers an adventure close to home for residents of the Midwest, as well as some world-class hiking destinations that draw backpackers from all over the country and beyond.

Those who find their way to the North Country Trail—whether long-distance hikers or day hikers or something in between—discover a different kind of experience. Hikers who have completed the entire route describe a trail with a completely different character than the conquer-the-mountain aesthetic of the big north–south Triple Crown routes. Perhaps the divergence of cultures and trail environments that makes this trail so hard to pigeonhole keeps it interesting and surprising. Too, the combination of backwoods experiences and interactions with small-town America adds a more substantial human element to the trail than is found on the more remote western trails.

PREVIOUS SPREAD: Rural scene along the Finger Lakes Trail section of the NCT, Tuller Hill State Forest, New York

OPPOSITE: View from Treadway Mountain, Adirondack Mountains, New York

It's also an easier trail to walk on, which is no small advantage when you are looking at a 4,600-mile journey. This is a landscape that was repeatedly flattened by the advance and retreat of Ice Age glaciers, so its mountains are modest, although the Sawtooths (Minnesota), the Porcupines (Michigan's Upper Peninsula), the Allegheny Ridge (Pennsylvania and southwestern New York), and even the lower sections of the Adirondack Park (where the route currently passes) offer both good workouts and good panoramas. As a result, hikers can slip into a rhythmic, meditative pace. It is a smoother passage through a gentler landscape.

Gentler does not mean boring. What the trail lacks in high mountains, it makes up for in lakes: literally thousands of them, many formed by glaciers, are found along the trail, not to mention the Great Lakes themselves. Waterfalls are another feature in the Boundary Waters Canoe Area Wilderness (Minnesota), on the Superior Hiking Trail (Minnesota), along the Finger Lakes Trail (New York), and in Hocking Hills State Park (Ohio). Continuing the water theme, the trail follows and crosses hundreds of rivers, from the headwaters of the St. Croix to the Ohio River, along with canals that were instrumental in America's expansion to the west.

Also important in the development of the north-country economy were the old-growth forests that once covered the region. Today, the majority of the forests are second growth, logging being one of the primary economic activities in the North Country, but some tracts of old-growth forest remain along the trail, their thick trunks and deep shades reminding hikers of an older and wilder America. Tallgrass prairie takes over in North Dakota, offering hikers the experience of seeing some of the last remaining inland seas of grass that once supported millions of bison. And punctuating the walk throughout are the towns and cities of the upper Midwest, where the trail takes on a more urban vibe.

This variety is what makes the North Country Trail a bit of a microcosm, unique in the American recreation mosaic. The American idea of wilderness pits man against nature, reserving wilderness as a place where man is a visitor but does not remain. NCT hikers walk through a settled landscape, perhaps more akin to the national parks of Europe, where backcountry and nature exist in tandem with towns and villages, grazing lands and farms. The combination of remote backwoods and settlements that change color and character as one moves from east to west makes for a trail that boasts variety—in some ways, perhaps the most variety of any of the national scenic trails, if not in terms of environmental extremes, then in terms of geography and human settlement.

BUILDING A MEGATRAIL

The North Country Trail was one of the original 14 trails named in the 1968 National Trails System Act as being worthy of study and possible inclusion in the system. The NCT study was launched in 1973 by a combined federal-state task force. One of the people working on the project was a college graduate, Tom Gilbert, who ran the show from its inception until his recent retirement as superintendent of the North Country Trail for the National Park Service.

The trail was added to the National Trails System by Congress in 1980. The North Country Trail Association was formed in 1981; today, its volunteers currently donate more than 75,000 hours a year to the trail. The route has continued to evolve through the process, expanding to 4,600 miles and stretching across seven states and 12 national forests. Easily accessible to the cities of the upper Midwest, the trail is less than a two- or three-hour drive from Albany, Buffalo, Pittsburgh, Cleveland, Dayton, Detroit, Minneapolis–St. Paul, Fargo, and others.

Had this trail been conceived, as was the Appalachian Trail, in the 1920s, its narrative might be quite different. In a time of smaller populations and simpler legalities, routing a trail through a farmer's field meant a handshake, not an official easement and incomprehensible contracts. Today's world is more complex, the pressures on the land are greater, and the legal ramifications—everything from tax benefits of easements to liability and negligence to the fear of conflict between recreational and commercial land use—loom larger. So, like other trails more recently conceived, the North Country Trail involves both backcountry and settled communities. Planning it must take both sets of interests into account.

Population density along the trail varies. For much, though not all, of its length, the NCT stays well north of the major metropolitan centers of the Northeast and the Midwest. Unlike a 12,000-foot rocky mountaintop, this is land that can be—and is being—used for all manner of purposes. In the trail's northern reaches, farming and logging and mining

remain primary land uses, along with tourism. In recent years, the resurgence of oil and natural gas drilling has occurred in some areas through which the trail passes. In North Dakota, even the most populous parts of the state seem vast and isolated, but the wide empty plains support farms and livestock. In its one major foray south of the northern population centers, the trail dips south of Detroit and Cleveland into Ohio, to more densely populated communities, some of which are in the path of suburbanization. The denser the population, the more shopping and strip malls; the more expensive the land, the less wild the landscape—and the more difficult it is to route a national scenic trail.

The problems of routing begin at the beginning: an example is the eastern terminus, currently at Crown Point, New York. The original hope for the North Country Trail was that it would start at a junction with the Appalachian Trail via Vermont's Long Trail. The Long Trail would then be a connector between the north–south Appalachian Trail and the east–west North Country Trail. That sounds simple enough—hike from Georgia to Vermont, hang a left, and continue to North Dakota. In the early days of the Appalachian Trail, grand dreams such as these were met with enthusiasm. Back then, AT organizers partnered with local trail clubs, including the Green Mountain Club. Indeed, the earliest miles designated as part of the Appalachian Trail were already existing footpaths on other trail systems, including the Long Trail.

In today's more complex world, Long Trail managers were at first reluctant to become part of a project that could bring yet more users to an already popular trail. So the current terminus of the North Country Trail—on a bridge that crosses Lake Champlain and goes into Vermont—does not currently connect with the Long Trail. The issue, however, has recently been revived, and trail managers of both systems and on both sides of the state line are studying how best to link the two trails. Official approval of the final plan and congressional approval are the next steps in the process. Already, however, hikers are going all the way to the AT at Maine Junction, Vermont, and calling it all the NCT.

Immediately west of the terminus, even more issues rear up to confront both trail managers and hikers. Crown Point is an interesting enough place to declare a terminus. Its two forts, built in the early

OPPOSITE: The Finger Lakes Trail, Mariposa State Forest, New York

FOLLOWING SPREAD: The NCT through Finger Lakes vineyards, New York (top left); a shelter along the Finger Lakes section of the NCT, Burt Hill State Forest, New York (bottom left); Rock City State Forest, New York (right)

1700s, were important Revolutionary War sites, with a strategic location on Lake Champlain. In fact, it was the birthplace of the US Navy, which fought its first engagement on the lake in 1776. But once hikers leave the park, there is not yet a trail to follow.

Here, too, the issue is one of competing pressures on the land. A North Country Trail starting in northeastern New York must, by definition and the realities of geography, pass through the state-managed Adirondack Park region. The Adirondack Park is an unusual management zone in America. Unlike most American parks—but like many European national parks—it encompasses towns, roads, ski areas, logging areas, farms, recreation areas, and mountain wildernesses. Reasonably accessible to the New York and Montreal metropolitan areas, the region booms with tourism and second-home development. The Adirondack Park, at more than six million acres, is in fact larger than Yellowstone National Park—although, unlike Yellowstone, these six million acres include three million acres under private ownership, 130,000 residents, 4,154 miles of public roads, and 500 miles of railroads, as well as towns, villages, ski areas, and sawmills. Land managers, local leaders, and environmentalists all have different concerns about the environmental and economic impact of new uses, such as the route of the NCT.

In the case of most national scenic trails, routing decisions are almost always made with iconic landscapes in mind. It's impossible to imagine the Appalachian Trail without the Great Smoky Mountains, the Shenandoah, and the high peaks of the Presidential Range; the same is true of the Pacific Crest Trail's string of bucket-list-worthy western destinations. True, a few land-management units have successfully resisted being included in a national scenic trail or have altered the exact routing for environmental, wildlife, land-management, practical, or other reasons. But for the most part, the great places *near* the trail system are *in* the system.

Not so in the Adirondacks: so far, management issues surrounding perceived overuse of the High Peaks region have not only kept the planned route south of the region's most popular beauty spots, but have also delayed a trail-routing decision. The result for hikers is that once they leave Crown Point, their first 150 miles will be on a patchwork of trails and roads on a route they make up themselves, with help from the North Country Trail Association.

And in a way, this encapsulates the issues faced by the trail as a whole: it is difficult to route thousands of miles of continuous footway through landscapes facing conflicts of development, ecological preservation, traditional rural industries, and tourism. It is not an optimal start for a 4,600-mile thru-hike. But in an inconvenient sort of way, it illustrates the very real challenges that any new long-distance trail faces.

Today's North Country Trail is very much a work in progress, with any description containing such hopeful caveats as "When completed, the trail will run . . . " and "Hikers will find . . . " Currently, just more than 2,701 miles of the trail are completed and reserved for hikers, additional routing is on roads that skirt private property, some of the trail is open to multiple-recreation use, and some of it passes through lands used for other purposes, most often farming and forestry, but also mining, grazing, and other residential and commercial uses.

This is not a trail to escape from settled America; it is a trail to see what rural America has been—and what it is becoming.

THE ROUTE

After its start at New York's Crown Point State Historic Site and the first 150 miles of temporary routing through the southern Adirondack Mountains south of the High Peaks, the trail settles down to business in central New York, where it enters canal country and follows paths along the Black River and Erie Canal. The route here is a mixture of trails and roads, interrupted by a few historic sites, including Fort Stanwix, dating to the Revolutionary War, and Erie Canal Village, where visitors can ride on a canal boat.

For the next 460 miles, from central to western New York, the North Country Trail is mostly contiguous with the Finger Lakes Trail, looping south around the Finger Lakes region and paralleling the Pennsylvania border until reaching New York's Allegany State Park. Marked trail leads through Allegany County in a forested landscape of glacier-created hills, lakes, valleys, and waterfalls.

Crossing into Pennsylvania, the trail enters the differently spelled but scenically similar Allegheny National Forest, where it spends about 100 miles heading southwest, neatly avoiding the Buffalo-Erie-Cleveland metropolis to the north. For about half of the Pennsylvania mileage, the path is fairly continuous

FOLLOWING SPREAD: The NCT heading toward Tionesta Scenic Area, Allegheny National Forest, Pennsylvania (left); fox, Allegheny National Forest, Pennsylvania (top right); porcupine, Allegheny National Forest, Pennsylvania (bottom right)

The North Country Trail

Approximately 4,600 miles from New York to North Dakota

- The North Country Trail
- Interstate Highway
- US Highway

N

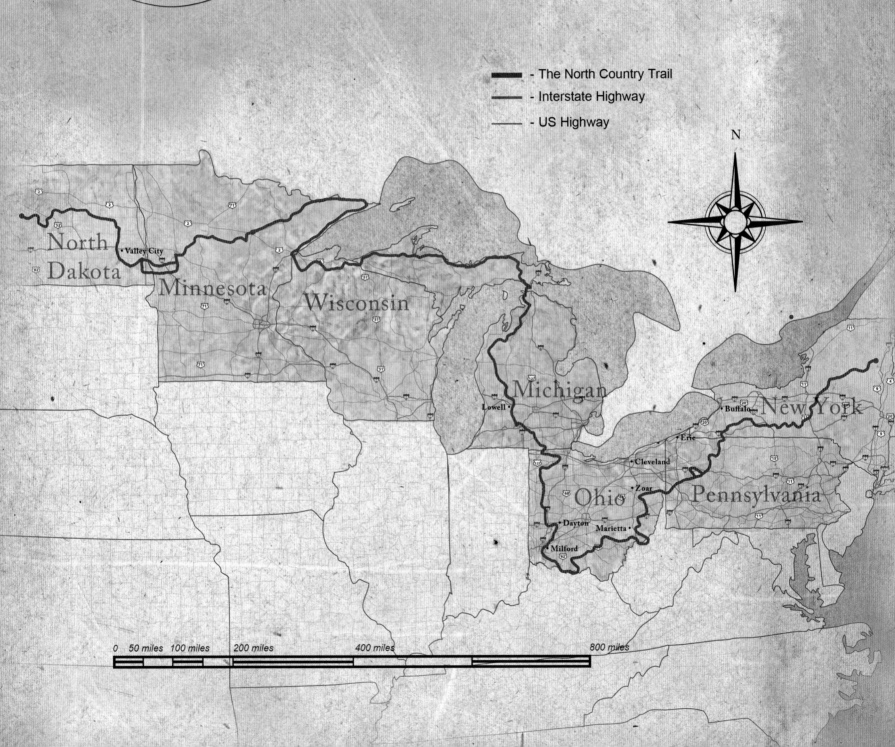

North Dakota

Valley City

Minnesota

Wisconsin

Michigan

Lowell

Buffalo

New York

Erie

Cleveland

Zoar

Ohio

Pennsylvania

Dayton

Marietta

Milford

0   50 miles   100 miles   200 miles   400 miles   800 miles

even as it picks its way through a jumble of state game lands, state parks, and private lands. Appalachian Trail hikers, rock hopping across the eastern side of the state, often refer to it as "Rocksylvania." The same name might be used here as hikers pass through Moraine State Park and Slippery Rock, whose boulders and ravines attest to the carving force of the glaciers. The last part of the state is a mix of designated trail and connectors.

In eastern Ohio, the North Country Trail continues its swing between public and private lands, old canals and historic sites, towns and suburbs, trails and road walking. Hikers who have driven across the state's less-than-exciting interstate highways might be surprised at the variety here, which includes a designated Wild and Scenic River, historic canals, Native American sites, and Underground Railroad stops. Here, the NCT meets another important goal of the National Trails System Act: to bring at least some parts of some trails to where people live and can easily access them. While this section of trail is far more popular with local residents than with out-of-state backpackers, hikers with specific interests in American history will find much to engage them here.

The first part of the Ohio section largely follows canal towpaths past some of the earliest settlements in the state. Near the village of Zoar, the North Country Trail picks up the Buckeye Trail, which it follows on a 993-mile arc on a 270-degree circumambulation of nearly two-thirds of the state. The forested, hilly eastern side of Ohio features trails along rivers and lakes. Highlights include Marietta—the first settlement in Ohio—and Hocking Hills State Park, an unexpected jewel of an outdoors destination, with sandstone cliffs, caves, and waterfalls.

History and prehistory continue to be a theme as the trail rounds the southern curve of the state. Some of the land is owned by the Ohio Historical Society, and two pre-Columbian sites—Fort Hill and the Serpent Mound—are located right on the NCT. Another noteworthy spot is Milford, where 22,000 miles of recreational trails intersect, including the American Discovery Trail, the Ohio to Erie Trail, the Underground Railroad Trail, the Little Miami Scenic Trail, and the Little Miami River Water Trail, not to mention the Buckeye Trail, the Sea-to-Sea Route (a routing from the Atlantic to the Pacific that encompasses the North Country Trail), and the NCT itself. From here, you truly can walk to anywhere.

From Dayton, the trail continues its same patchwork character: here a road walk, there a sidewalk, here a rail trail, there a bike path. The Miami and Erie Canal Towpath and the Wabash Cannonball Rail Trail provide much of the footway as the North Country Trail leaves the Buckeye Trail and heads north to the Michigan border.

The northbound trail through the lower part of Michigan continues much in the same vein. Stretches of completed, certified footway alternate with a mix of forest, farm, and country roads. In Lowell, hikers walk right past the North Country Trail Association headquarters (souvenirs, maps, and memberships are available). As it moves north and the population becomes sparser, the trail begins to offer more of a backcountry experience, with much of it completed. Marked trail goes through the Manistee National Forest, followed by new trail sections along the Hodenpyl Dam Pond and the Manistee River, and then the Jordan River Pathway and the lakeside route through Wilderness State Park on Lake Michigan.

Now in northern Lower Michigan, the trail is fully in the cold-weather corridor—the true North Country—where sticking snows blow off the Great Lakes starting in mid-November and last into April. (And that's just the start: winter is even longer and whiter in some sections of Minnesota and North Dakota yet ahead.) Much of the trail here is used by snowshoers and cross-country skiers. Brilliant fall foliage makes autumn a beautiful hiking season, with the peak running from late September through mid-October; however, fall is also hunting season, so hikers should wear bright safety-orange vests, hats, and pack covers. Early summer belongs to the mosquitoes and blackflies.

The Mackinac Bridge links the upper and lower peninsulas of Michigan. The bridge is open to pedestrians only for a Labor Day morning walk; the other 364 days of the year, a shuttle can be arranged for those on foot. In the Upper Peninsula, the trail takes on a completely different character—wild and remote. This is an outdoor destination that people travel from all over the Midwest to experience. Much of the trail is completed, although there are still quite a few road connectors. Shaded by old-growth forests, following along the Lake Superior shoreline, the trail goes through Tahquamenon Falls State Park, which boasts one of the largest waterfalls in the eastern United States; Pictured Rocks National Lakeshore; and several

OPPOSITE: Remnants of an old mill, State Game Land 283, Pennsylvania (top); McConnells Mill State Park, Pennsylvania (bottom)

FOLLOWING SPREAD: Slippery Rock Creek Gorge, McConnells Mill State Park, Pennsylvania (left); Natural Bridge, Wayne National Forest, Ohio (right)

designated wilderness areas, city and state parks, state forests, and national forests. The Upper Peninsula stretch of trail ends in the Porcupine Mountains Wilderness State Park, widely considered one of the best hiking destinations in the upper Midwest.

One of Wisconsin's claims to fame (besides cheese curds and the Packers) is that it hosts more national scenic trail mileage than any other state in the nation. Not only does the North Country Trail traverse northern Wisconsin, but the 1,200-mile Ice Age Trail winds its way from the north to the south, then back up and across the state in a giant serpentine.

However, Wisconsin's NCT spends plenty of time on connector segments, both on its eastern and western ends. The first, albeit short, finished backcountry trail segments in Wisconsin are in the Penokee Mountains of Iron County Forest. And just past waterfall-rich Copper Falls State Park, an almost continuous stretch of backcountry trail runs west for 120 miles through the Chequamegon-Nicolet National Forest, which includes the Porcupine Lake Wilderness and the Rainbow Lake Wilderness. Marked trail continues through the red and white pine forests of Bayfield County Forest, followed by Brule River State Forest, with scenic bluffs over the Bois Brule River, the Historic Portage Trail—which commemorates the explorers, fur traders, and settlers of the north woods—and the roughly half-mile boardwalk over the Brule Bog. The Douglas County Wildlife Area—a pine barrens—is the last large stretch of finished trail in the state. From here on, the North Country Trail route zigs and zags northwest often on long stretches of straight-line paved roads. It passes the St. Croix National Scenic Riverway, one of only three national parks on or alongside the entire trail, and reaches the Minnesota border about a half mile south of Jay Cooke State Park.

Minnesota boasts outdoor areas that draw visitors from all over the country: the Superior Hiking Trail and the Boundary Waters Canoe Area Wilderness are world-class destinations. This trail section (the so-called "Arrowhead Re-route," encompassing the Superior, Border Route, and Kekekabic Hiking Trails) is not yet officially on the NCT, as it was not included in the trail's original comprehensive plan. It must be approved by Congress before being formally added to the official NCT. In the meantime, hikers more interested in superlative wilderness experiences than bureaucratic processes use it, as

this 400-mile stretch of finished, marked hiking trail offers some of the best hiking in the Midwest, and indeed, on the entire North Country Trail. Entering Minnesota, hikers jump on the 280-mile Superior Hiking Trail, then take the Border Route Trail near the US-Canadian border through the Boundary Waters Canoe Area Wilderness, followed by the Kekekabic Trail. For thru-hikers, the only unsettling aspect of the famed walk along the shore of Lake Superior is that it heads in a northeasterly direction, whereas the goal—North Dakota—lies firmly to the west. The detour, however, is worth the extra miles.

About 130 miles of road walking then leads to the Chippewa National Forest, the next section of designated trail, a 70-mile stretch followed by another approximately 100-mile patchwork of short designated trail sections alternating with country roads through lake country to the North Dakota border.

Finally, North Dakota: this is where the definition of a North Country landscape changes yet again. In this northern prairie, seas of grass undulate to a far horizon, the fields carpeted in spring and summer with wildflowers. Land that once was home to millions of bison now has one of the most important waterfowl nesting sites in North America.

The trail through the state bounces between undesignated road walking and designated trail. In the eastern part of the state, it passes Fort Abercrombie State Historic Site and the Sheyenne National Grasslands, the largest remaining remnant of tallgrass prairie in public ownership. Here, the NCT follows the banks of the Sheyenne River, which it continues to do through much of the state. A 30-mile stretch of designated trail north of Valley City along Lake Ashtabula is followed by another patchwork of roads, although this open, sparsely settled country is a far cry from walking through the more developed road stretches of the lower Midwest. Roadside panoramas and points of interest include prairie pothole wetlands, riverside forests, glacially formed hills, fields of wildflowers, and Native American cultural sites, plus examples of current economic uses of the land: pastures for both cattle and buffalo and farm fields growing canola, sunflowers, wheat, and sugar beets. The western 200 miles of trail is almost finished, including a stretch through the Lake Audubon National Wildlife Refuge, with the exception of the trail immediately adjacent to the NCT's western terminus in Lake Sakakawea State Park.

OPPOSITE: Ash Cave, Hocking Hills State Park, Ohio

FOLLOWING SPREAD: The NCT through Manistee National Forest, Michigan (left); rural scene near Eagle Mills, Ohio (top right); a cat in front of Fraker Mill Covered Bridge, along the Wabash Cannonball Trail section of the NCT, Ohio (middle right); remnants of a lock along the Miami and Erie Canal, Ohio (bottom right)

PREVIOUS SPREAD: Island Lake, Paul Bunyan State Forest, Minnesota (left); the NCT through a birch forest, Itasca State Park, Minnesota (right)

LEFT: Fort Abercrombie State Historic Site, North Dakota (top); Viking statue at Fort Ransom State Park, Sheyenne River Valley, North Dakota (bottom)

OPPOSITE: Sheyenne Lake, Lonetree Wildlife Management Area, North Dakota

THE NORTH COUNTRY TRAIL

To try to pick 10 or so highlights from a trail that is 4,600 miles long is an almost impossible task. With the help of Ron Strickland, author of *The North Country Trail: The Best Walks, Hikes, and Backpacking Trips on America's Longest National Scenic Trail,* this list presents notable hikes that showcase a representative variety of the different landscapes awaiting NCT hikers.

WATKINS GLEN (New York)

A 10-mile mostly downhill hike from Sugar Hill State Forest to Watkins Glen State Park begins with a fire tower with sweeping views. Located where the North Country Trail shares its tread with the Finger Lakes Trail, it passes lean-tos (ideal for lunch breaks), ruins of early settlements (ideal for ghost stories), a waterfall (ideal for cooling off), and a lovely creekside walk (ideal for daydreaming). The hike ends at the town of Watkins Glen, one of rural New York's premier tourist destinations.

HELLS HOLLOW (Pennsylvania)

This 7.7-mile hike from Alpha Pass to Hells Hollow is a trip through glacier-scoured terrain. It alternates between following the creekside of Slippery Rock Creek with roiling Class III and Class IV rapids, and climbing atop the surrounding ravine for views. A covered bridge, a working gristmill from the 19th century, and an extra half-mile trail to Hell Run complete the journey.

HOCKING HILLS STATE PARK (Ohio)

This state park is a surprising outdoor recreation jewel for the Midwest. The secret is out; Hocking Hills has become Ohio's premier outdoor destination, with waterfalls, caves, bluffs, hemlock forests, a network of trails, zip lines, and kayaking. The six-mile Grandma Gatewood Trail memorializes the Ohio grandmother who became the first solo woman to thru-hike the Appalachian Trail, and was cofounder of the Buckeye Trail Association.

SHAWNEE STATE FOREST (Ohio)

Dixie (complete with umbrella magnolia and other plants more common to southern climes) meets North Country in this southern section of the NCT near the Kentucky border, where the mild climate supports an ecosystem rarely seen anywhere north of the Mason-Dixon Line. Going from Forest Road 6 to State Road 125, the hike is mostly downhill. A nature center offers interpretive programs.

LAKE SUPERIOR SHORELINE (Michigan)

This 5.6-mile hike from Muskallonge Lake to Perrys Landing near Grand Marais, Michigan, is a coastal walk along Lake Superior. Beach walking, pine forests, and blueberries in season during July and August are some of the features here.

PICTURED ROCKS (Michigan)

This is a full-fledged multiday backpack trip on the 43-mile Lakeshore Trail along the Lake Superior Shore on the Upper Peninsula. With its bluffs and beaches, it is one of the greatest hits of the entire North Country Trail.

BRULE BOG (Wisconsin)

Two short out-and-back day hikes starting at the Upper St. Croix Lake trailhead turn hikers with imaginations into Native Americans, fur traders, explorers, or settlers who used the portage here to cross from the Great Lakes to the Mississippi watersheds. One of the walks is a .7-mile boardwalk (wheelchair accessible) built over Brule Bog's white cedar swamp.

SUPERIOR–BOUNDARY WATERS CANOE AREA–KEKEKABIC SECTION (Minnesota)

This 400-mile section of completed (but not yet designated) trail is some of the best long-distance hiking not only on the NCT, but also in the country. It is currently under study for inclusion in the NCT, and is described in *Guide to the Superior Hiking Trail* (Superior Hiking Trail Association) and *Border Route Trail Guide* (Border Route Trail Association).

ITASCA MORAINE CHAIN OF LAKES (Minnesota)

More than 25 kettle lakes formed when glacial ice blocks, trapped under sand and glacial

debris, melted. A 10-mile hike heading west from the Nelson Lake Campground follows an old railroad bed and old logging roads past ponds and lakes typical of the Minnesota North Country.

SHEYENNE NATIONAL GRASSLANDS
(North Dakota)

The tallgrass prairies that stretched beyond the farthest horizon of a wide-open country are rare today, but hikers walk through a sampling at the Sheyenne National Grasslands. In spring and summer—and even fall—there is plenty of color as grassland flowers take their turns in bloom.

Top Left: The NCT through Sheyenne National Grasslands; *Top Right:* Chapel Rock, Pictured Rocks National Lakeshore; *Bottom:* Walkway through a deeply eroded gorge, Watkins Glen State Park

THE ICE AGE TRAIL

➤ WATER, GRAVITY, COLD, AND TIME ◄

Among the beauty spots along the national scenic trails—iconic mountains such as Rainier, Whitney, Washington, and Katahdin, parks such as Grand Canyon, Yellowstone, and Yosemite—the gentle rolling fields and forests of Wisconsin may seem something of a misfit. It is a pretty land with neat farms, sparkling lakes, forests full of birdsong. But it seems hardly dramatic enough to be in the same league as the more famous national scenic trails. That is, unless you can read the secret history that is engraved in these hills and forests. Then, the Ice Age Trail—a 1,200-mile route that arcs and wiggles through Wisconsin—might just have one of the most dramatic stories of all. • The Ice Age Trail is one of only three national scenic trails to be contained within a single state. It is also the only national scenic trail dedicated to a geological event, in this case telling a story of the sheer power of ice, water, and erosion.

Interestingly, the other two national scenic trails contained within single states can also be said to have something of a water theme: The Florida Trail, with its swamps, marshes, and the occasional alligator, is at least in part a trail about too much water. The Arizona Trail, a sere and parched landscape of shimmering heat waves, is about too little.

The Ice Age Trail is about the mighty force of water. Here, the terrain shows the effects of the land-carving power of glacial ice, the torrential rains and snows, the grinding of rocks transported hundreds of miles by ice moving in answer to the inexorable call of gravity, the sculpting power of drops of water dribbling one at a time over centuries. The story tells of nothing less than a cataclysm, slow moving but unstoppable, that took place over thousands of years and etched a record on the land. For those who can read it, the Ice Age Trail is a story of one of America's great geological events, writ large in a landscape whose gentle appearance belies its tumultuous formation.

Some facts set the stage: The Ice Age occurred as a series of cooling-and-warming cycles that took place over the last two million years. (Some geologists speculate that the planet may currently be in a warming period between ice ages, and that another glaciation could be in the future, perhaps thousands—or tens of thousands—of years hence.) Each time the cooling cycle began, glaciers expanded and crept down from the north, obliterating landforms in their path. When the climate warmed, they melted and receded, leaving behind the detritus of their mighty movement—rocks, sand, gravel, hills, depressions, and rich fertile farmland. Sometimes, the meltwater flooded, carving new channels through lands previously unaffected by the glaciers. In the next cycle, the glaciers crept back again, once more leveling and scouring, and then retreating. In Wisconsin, that last cooling cycle—now called the Wisconsin Glaciation—took place between 85,000 and 10,000 years ago. At its apex, perhaps 25,000 to 20,000 years ago, it covered roughly two-thirds of the state.

Ice sheets, or glaciers, are part of the topography of the globe: the National Snow and Ice Data Center estimates that even today 99 percent of the world's fresh water is contained within massive ice sheets that cover Antarctica and Greenland. Ice sheets and glaciers are permanent (though currently shrinking) features of Arctic and Antarctic climes. Elsewhere, glaciers may escape their latitudinal prisons to reside at high elevations. In North America during the Ice Age, cooler temperatures at lower latitudes enabled glaciers to expand far to the south.

It is the sheer scale of the Ice Age glaciation that boggles the mind. Imagine an ice sheet between a half mile and a mile thick. Comparisons help: A mile high is nearly four times the height of the Willis (formerly Sears) Tower in Chicago. A mile deep is the depth of the Grand Canyon. Now, imagine a sheet of ice big enough to cover the Willis Tower four times over, or fill the Grand Canyon. Imagine it covering most of the state of Wisconsin, along with much of today's Midwest and Northeast—oh, and also, all of Canada.

And then imagine all that ice moving. The motion is caused by a combination of gravity and cooling temperatures. As temperatures to the south dropped, the climate became cool enough that more snow fell than could melt. As more and more and more snow fell, gravity pushed it downward, and the combination of the downward force with the melting and freezing cycle turned the snow into something that had the consistency of frozen chunky molasses—much like the artificial snow on a ski slope is different from the natural snow on top of it. The crumbling melted and refrozen snow at the edges of the glacier started falling in a sort of slow-motion torrent. As the glaciers expanded and moved to the south, they picked up and carried huge hunks of rock and tiny specks of sand, as well as boulders, smaller rocks and cobbles, and chunks of metal and clay. The combination of icy crystals and hard rock scoured the land, leaving debris hither and yon, flinging boulders this way and that. When, finally, the ice melted during a period of warming, the glacier left all that debris (called "drift") on the land, creating a variety of formations and flat outwash plains. The end moraine—the ridge of hills marking the farthest advance of the last ice sheet to cover Wisconsin—is what forms the landscape of the Ice Age Trail.

THE GIFTS OF THE GLACIERS

Today's hiker, perhaps knowing little about glacially created landscapes, might at first miss some of the evidence of the cataclysm that once occurred on the land and completely reshaped it. Unlike the results of tectonic and volcanic action, the results of glaciation are not sky-piercing pinnacles, but rather a subtler sort of land remodeling. Much of it is obscured by grass and leaves and farm crops—the perfectly ordinary things you can see everywhere in the largely gentle Midwest.

PREVIOUS SPREAD: Sturgeon Bay, Lake Michigan

OPPOSITE: The IAT through a cedar forest in Potawatomi State Park

FOLLOWING SPREAD: Fishing boat along Algoma waterfront, Forestville segment of the IAT (top left); Rawley Point Lighthouse, Point Beach State Park (bottom left); Lake Michigan along Point Beach State Park (right)

So a more nearsighted focus is needed to see that something here is a bit different. The scale is morphed; something is slightly jarring—odd, off-kilter—about the landforms. Beneath the fields and farms are distinctive formations: A squiggly ridge looks like it might have been made by a monster-sized earthworm burrowing just beneath the surface. A series of teardrop-shaped hills all point the same way, lined up like soldiers. Little cones look like miniature volcanoes. A perfectly round lake is dug into the ground, surrounded by rock fields that look like they might have been put there by giants. An armchair-sized rock, resembling nothing else nearby, sits all by itself in the middle of a field.

These features, with names as unfamiliar as their shapes—eskers, drumlins, kames, kettles, erratics—might be unremarkable, if, indeed, they were even noticed among the show-off spires of, say, the Rocky Mountains. But they are evidence of enormous forces: the work of ice, snow, water, gravity, and ultimately, of heat, which melted the glaciers and left only these comparatively minute remains as evidence of what once was. No longer able to observe the glaciers, unable to fully imagine them, one can only surmise about the size and scope of the ice sheet that left these landforms behind.

Hikers walking along the Ice Age Trail might consider that the surrounding scenery could be called the trash heap of the gods—the junk that remained when some ancient geological Ice Queen retreated to her northern homeland. Other landscapes in the National Scenic Trails System were created by geologic temper tantrums, by explosive, fiery forces beneath the surface that moved the earth with plate tectonics, hot spots, and volcanism. This landscape was created by a cold, icy fury: a force on the surface that carried and piled stones and rocks as part of a gravity-fueled process of movement and scouring.

Eskers, for instance—those ridges that look like they were made by giant earthworms pushing up from below the surface—are actually filled-in tunnels that were formed by water flowing at the very bottom of thousands of feet of ice. In something like a lost-wax process, meltwater dripped to the bottom of the ice sheet, to the place where ice met land, and then flowed underneath the glacier, carving tunnels in the ice following the path of least resistance. The flowing water carried with it sand and rock freed from the ice by the melting; this debris was deposited in the tunnel.

When the ice above melted, all the rock and dirt and sand and refuse it carried was left behind in those tunnels, creating the long, narrow ridges. For the hiker today, eskers are long, thin heights of land from which to survey the bumps and creases left by the glaciers—and from which to see the distinct divide between the land to the north, which was once covered by the ice sheet, and the land to the south, which was not.

Or take the little kames—cones—perhaps 250 feet high, which look like child-sized volcanoes. These kames are piles of rubble that accumulated as water dripped straight down through a fracture in the ice sheet. When the water moved on, it left the rubble behind. Nothing more than another geological garbage heap, really, these little bumps give shape and contour to a landscape where a downhill ski area with fewer than 500 feet of vertical elevation gain may even have the word "Mount" in its name.

Kettles are another telltale sign of glaciation. These mostly small-sized lakes began as chunks of ice that broke off the main body of the glacier, became buried in glacial debris, and then became depressions when they melted. Some of these are dry, but many became the small, shallow bodies of water that form the majority of Wisconsin's more than 15,000 lakes.

Some of Wisconsin's larger bodies of water are also the result of glaciation; for example, Horicon Marsh, an important wetland and flyway for migrating and marsh birds today, traces its ancestry back to a proglacial lake. So does today's Wisconsin River with its famous scenic dells—a gorge cut through sandstone rock estimated to be perhaps 500,000,000 years old, exposed and carved by the melting waters of the retreating glacier. Although this region of Wisconsin is part of the so-called Driftless Area, a section that was never covered by the glacier, the glacier affected it nonetheless when proglacial Lake Wisconsin flooded and breached its ice dam. Geologists believe that the resulting deluge cut through the ancient sandstone and created the buttes and bluffs of the Wisconsin Dells in a matter of days.

This is, in short, a landscape that is more than meets the eye. John Muir, the Scottish-born wilderness advocate and Sierra Club cofounder, who is most closely associated with the High Sierra, grew up near today's Ice Age Trail in Wisconsin after immigrating to America as a child. A portion of the Ice Age Trail now winds through what was Fountain Lake Farm, Muir's family home in Marquette County; it's now a

OPPOSITE: Distant kames from Parnell Tower, Kettle Moraine State Forest (top); Carmelite monastery atop Holy Hill, Holy Hill segment of the IAT (bottom)

county memorial park named after him. Also commemorating the state's adopted son is a network of eponymous biking and hiking trails in the southern unit of the Kettle Moraine State Forest, which links up with the Ice Age Trail.

A TRAIL ALONG ICE AGE REMAINS

Like so many of the national scenic trails, the Ice Age Trail began as the long-term passion of one man, in this case, Milwaukee native Ray Zillmer. With the goal of establishing a national park following the line of the last glaciation in Wisconsin, Zillmer founded the Ice Age Park and Trail Foundation (now the Ice Age Trail Alliance) in 1958. The alliance spent the next 20 years working with volunteers to study trail routes, measure mileages, and plan connecting routes.

In 1964, the Ice Age National Scientific Reserve system was created by an Act of Congress, comprising nine separate units, each of which represented a different facet of the glaciation, ranging from marshes to hilltop prairies. Administered by the state of Wisconsin, with the assistance of the National Park Service, these nine reserves provide a portrait of the Wisconsin Glaciation. Six of them are on the Ice Age Trail; the others are in the general region of the trail.

The idea of an Ice Age Trail was picked up and supported by the late Wisconsin congressman Henry S. Reuss, who in 1976 authored the book *On the Trail*

of the Ice Age. The Ice Age Trail was authorized as a national scenic trail by Congress in 1980, and was named a state scenic trail in 1987.

The Ice Age Trail is administered at the federal level by the National Park Service, which works in partnership with the Wisconsin Department of Natural Resources, the Ice Age Trail Alliance, and local partners to plan the route of the trail, acquire lands on which to establish it, and assemble and allocate the resources necessary to construct and maintain it. Much of the on-the-ground work is carried out by volunteers recruited and coordinated by the alliance.

The goal is a trail that, when complete, will run some 1,200 miles from the eastern part of the state in Door County to the Minnesota border. Approximately 600 miles are currently in place, with more being added. Most of the completed segments (marked with yellow blazes) are set aside for hiking and backpacking (and, in winter, cross-country skiing and snowshoeing), with bicycle, horse, and motorized use allowed only on a few sections of trail where those uses have been historically permitted. The remaining 600 miles are "connecting routes"—unblazed paths typically along quiet country roads that are suggested by the Ice Age Trail Alliance as a way to help long-distance hikers connect the established segments of trail. In some cases, connectors are bike paths; in other cases, they may be sidewalks that wander through small Wisconsin towns. Sometimes, the connectors and undesignated footpaths follow old trails that have been poorly maintained and are blocked by blowdowns and other damage, making them difficult to follow and hike through.

During hunting season, hikers share much of the trail with hunters and fishermen—land uses that certainly date back to the Ice Age. Early Native Americans followed game across the Bering Strait, then migrated ahead of the encroaching ice. But the wildlife they were following was very different than what one sees today. It was an age of wildlife that was every bit as overscaled and oversized as the massive glaciers that flowed out of the north: now-extinct megafauna included woolly mammoths and mastodons, along with giant beavers that could weigh as much as 200 pounds, stag-moose, and piglike peccaries. Today's animal inventory includes beavers, badgers, raccoons, wolves, red foxes, white-tailed deer, black bears, turkeys, and sandhill cranes. The

BELOW: Painted turtles in Silver Creek, West Bend segment of the IAT

OPPOSITE: An esker along the Loew Lake segment of the IAT

The Ice Age Trail

Approximately 1,200 miles from Green Bay to the Wisconsin-Minnesota border

- The Ice Age Trail
- Interstate Highway
- US Highway

N

0 25 miles 50 miles 100 miles 150 miles 200 miles

Bayfield
Ashland
2
Mason
Hurley
Solon Springs
Mellen
53
63
51
Hayward
Butternut
Eagle River
Webster
Spooner
45
Grantsburg
Couderay
Phillips
Rhinelander
Crandon
8
Balsam Lake
Rice Lake
Kennan
8
Weyerhaeuser
8
Oscenda
Sheldon
Rib Lake
Crivitz
Prairie Farm
Merrill
Antigo
White Lake
New Richmond
Bloomer
Lublin
Athens
51
River Falls
12
Colfax
Stanley
94
Eau Claire
Mosinee
Shawano
Plum City
Durand
12
Spencer
45
Granton
10
Iola
New London
Independence
Wisconsin Rapids
53
Black River Falls
Melrose
10
Potter
90
14
Norwalk
51
Wautoma
94
Berlin
La Farge
Montello
Fond du Lac
Portage
151
45
Baraboo
Clyman
Boscobel
14
Highland
Madison
94
Milwaukee
Lancaster
Darlington
Burlington
94

lakes and rivers are filled with muskie, northern pike, perch, smallmouth bass, walleye, and more. And, in a landscape created by ice, carved by water, and fueled by seasonal snows and snowmelt, there is an abundance—or more accurately, an overabundance—of the less-beloved sort of wildlife: mosquitoes and black-flies. In early summer, let the hiker beware!

THE ROUTE

The routing and construction of the Ice Age Trail has followed the same meandering and obstacle-strewn path (both literally and figuratively) as other long-distance trails, and with 600 miles still to go, much of the work still lies ahead. Complicating the picture is the fact that the Ice Age Trail lies a mere 20 miles from 60 percent of the state's population. Certainly, this is in line with one of the goals of the National Trails System Act, to put some sections of trails near cities and population centers. On the plus side, the trail serves a broad population and can draw upon that base for volunteers and supporters. But running through a populated area means that the route competes with other more lucrative land uses—from shopping malls to suburban developments to corporate offices to tourism hot spots—a problem it shares with other unfinished trails in the National Scenic Trails System. Wisconsin's Stewardship Program is a state program to assist in funding land acquisition and easement protection, and some federal monies are available from the National Park Service. But it could be decades before the entire trail is certified and protected.

None of this means that the full trail route—including unmarked connecting routes—isn't hikeable now. Although fewer than 100 people have reported thru-hiking the entire trail, the route does exist, and certified sections blazed with the trail's official emblem—a rounded triangle picturing a woolly mammoth—are found throughout the state. Thru-hikers typically start in August to avoid the worst of the mosquitoes; this schedule, however, puts hikers in the path of Wisconsin's enthusiastic autumn hunting season.

In the macro sense—and especially when compared to some of the longer mountainous national scenic trails with their greater changes in latitude and elevation—the route of the Ice Age Trail seems homogenous. The moderate changes in elevation and latitude mean that there are no great changes in climate, and for hikers, that makes for an easier hike to plan—no need for packing winter gear for one section and desert gear for the next. The hiking season is spring through fall, with much of the trail in winter available to snowshoers and cross-country skiers.

The Ice Age Trail makes an irregular U-shaped meander through Wisconsin, starting at Potawatomi State Park in the Door Peninsula at Sturgeon Bay (an inlet of Green Bay), then dipping south within an easy drive from Lake Michigan's shoreline communities, including Milwaukee. This first segment includes Kettle Moraine State Forest, which highlights some of the classic glacial landforms, not only the eponymous kettles and moraines, but eskers and kames as well. As hikers become attuned to the landscape, land features that formerly only registered as slight bumps now reveal their past as serendipitous creations formed from the battle between rock and ice, cold and gravity.

A little south of Milwaukee, the trail swings west, and cuts across the state close to the Illinois border. When it is just south of Madison, the trail makes a tight little dogleg, followed by a sharp turn to the north; it then cuts up the center of the state on the line between the glaciated region and the so-called Driftless Area near Baraboo. Here, the Wisconsin Dells, formed by a massive release of glacial meltwater, and Devils Lake State Park, a former river channel that was plugged by moraines, are among the state's most popular outdoor destinations.

The trail continues north, through less populated country, until it has just passed the latitude where it first started at Green Bay. Here, it makes one more sharp turn, this time to the west to pass through Chequamegon National Forest—characterized by boggy pathways, glacial ridges, kames, and kettles, all made more challenging by beaver dams that challenge the trail's routing and hikers' patience, sometimes on an annual basis. Muddy feet and mosquitoes in spring and early summer make late summer and fall the preferred hiking seasons. The trail then goes through the descriptively named Chippewa Moraine State Recreation Area (considered one of the most scenic hiking areas in the state) and after that reaches Interstate State Park on the Wisconsin-Minnesota border, where the trail ends at the Dalles of the St. Croix River. *Dalles*—the French word for the rapids of a river confined between the walls of a gorge or canyon—refers to the tempestuous river flowing between towering black cliffs formed, like the Wisconsin Dells, by the rapid release of a flood of water from a lake that was a precursor to Lake Superior.

PREVIOUS SPREAD: The IAT through Kettle Moraine State Forest (top and bottom left); Balanced Rock and Devils Lake, Devils Lake State Park (right)

FOLLOWING SPREAD: Oak trees, Mecan River segment of the IAT (top left); rural scene along the Sauk Point segment of the IAT near Parfreys Glen (middle left); northern river otter, Portage Canal segment of the IAT (bottom left); the Marquette segment of the IAT along Fox River (right)

OPPOSITE: Dells of the Eau Claire River

RIGHT: The Old Railroad segment of the IAT along Game Lake (top); a bench along the IAT, Chippewa Moraine Ice Age State Recreation Area (bottom)

FOLLOWING SPREAD: Forested glacial moraine along Trade River (left); Dalles of the St. Croix River (right)

THE ICE AGE TRAIL

In close tangent with the Ice Age Trail is the Ice Age National Scientific Reserve, which comprises nine sites near or right along the trail. These reserves have been chosen as landscapes that represent some of the most significant Ice Age–created landforms along the 1,200-mile route. At present, the reserves—most of which are in the state park system—range from full-fledged visitor centers to undeveloped sites where visitors are on their own. Taken together, they have the aim of protecting, preserving, and interpreting the most significant glacial features along and near the Ice Age Trail. Six are on the trail itself, three are near enough to be part of an outing to the trail, and, as a group, they represent the diverse glacial formations to be seen in Wisconsin.

TWO CREEKS BURIED FOREST

At Two Creeks Buried Forest, glacial silt covered a forest of black and white spruce, hemlock, and pine between 11,000 and 12,000 years ago; later, another glacier flattened the area, leaving behind a clay layer containing logs and debris. Today, layers of clay, silt, sand, and ancient forest can be seen on steep bluffs where the waves of Lake Michigan and erosion have unearthed the story beneath the dunes.

KETTLE MORAINE STATE FOREST

The trail runs through several districts of the Kettle Moraine State Forest, which actually comprises several disconnected land units spread over southeast Wisconsin. The Henry S. Reuss Ice Age Visitor Center in the northern unit is a starting point for understanding the glacial landforms. Built atop a kame, the lookout platform has views of an esker and another kame. Within a short drive are several moraines, and parks where camping, swimming, and boating are permitted.

CAMPBELLSPORT DRUMLINS

Not on the trail, but within a short drive of Kettle Moraine State Forest, the Campbellsport Drumlins showcase one of the oddest glacial landforms. Drumlins are tear-shaped mounds that all point the same way, indicating the direction of movement of the glacier that formed them. There is no interpretive center or publicly owned land here, but the drumlins are visible from the scenic drives in the area.

HORICON MARSH STATE WILDLIFE AREA

Horicon Marsh is not physically on the Ice Age Trail, but it is easily accessible from the Milwaukee area and southeastern Wisconsin. This extinct glacial lake—now a marsh—is one of the most important flyways for migrating birds in the upper Midwest. The northern two-thirds of the marsh is the Horicon National Wildlife Refuge.

CROSS PLAINS

Located just west of Madison near the village of Cross Plains on the very edge of the Driftless Area, this region provides a dramatic example of the difference between glaciated and unglaciated terrain. Glacier features include a glacial lake and a gorge carved by meltwater, and expansive views of both driftless and glaciated terrain. The Ice Age Complex at Cross Plains is a planned 1,600-acre compilation of federal, state, and county land preserving these landscape features. To date, 750 acres have been acquired.

DEVILS LAKE

Located three miles south of Baraboo and a few minutes' drive from the tourist attractions of the Wisconsin Dells, Devils Lake State Park is one of the most popular parks in the state. The lake was created when moraines of the glacier formed a dam at two ends of a deep river channel between high bluffs. The moraines are easily visible from trails atop the bluffs from which hikers enjoy excellent views. A series of interesting rock formations, including Balanced Rock, make scenic day-hike destinations. The Ice Age Trail makes a bit of a detour to visit Devils Lake, and it's worth the extra mileage to get there. Also available are a visitor's center, hiking trails, a swimming beach, boating, and camping.

MILL BLUFF STATE PARK

This park near Camp Douglas to the west of the Ice Age Trail contains the former islands and lake bed of Glacial Lake Wisconsin. The

prominent sandstone bluffs rise to heights between 80 and 200 feet, having formed as sea stacks in the middle of Glacial Lake Wisconsin. The steep formations were used as navigation landmarks during the early settlement of pioneers.

CHIPPEWA MORAINE STATE RECREATION AREA

This small scenic backcountry destination is mostly undeveloped, making it one of Wisconsin's secret hiking getaways. The area is filled with glacier-created landforms, such as kettle lakes and ponds, ice-walled lake plains, moraines, and hummocks. Ranger-led nature and wildlife walks make it a good destination for families.

INTERSTATE STATE PARK

On the Wisconsin-Minnesota border, this popular state park draws tourists with its camping, nonmotorized boating, trails, swimming, picnicking, and fishing, as well as its interpretive center, which showcases the region's geologic and natural history. Like the Dells of the Wisconsin River, the Dalles of the St. Croix are thought to have been formed when melting glaciers flooded, breaching the lake banks and carving a path through ancient stone.

TIMMS HILL

In addition to the scientific reserves listed above, the Ice Age Trail has another anomaly: it has one of only two national connecting trails, an odd little category in the National Trails System that was intended to recognize trails that connect a national scenic trail to a point of interest. The Ice Age Trail passes close to Timms Hill, the state's 1,952-foot high point in north-central Wisconsin, and this side trail leads from the Ice Age Trail to the modest summit. An observation tower at the top offers a bit more of a feeling of having climbed something high.

Top Left: The IAT along the Pike Lake unit of Kettle Moraine State Forest; *Top Right:* Snapping turtles along the Chippewa Moraine segment of the IAT

THE POTOMAC HERITAGE TRAIL

Within sight of Washington, DC, a paved footpath hugs the Virginia bank of the Potomac River, at first impression nothing more than an ordinary urban recreation trail. A Frisbee toss from the river, the trail is populated with weekend strollers, families, bicyclists, roller skaters, and, once in a blue moon, a hiker with a backpack. Very little in Washington is ordinary, and this footpath is no exception. • The city is framed by the extraordinary: a commuter's daily drive might cross the Francis Scott Key Bridge, or perhaps pass Arlington National Cemetery with its graves of heroes and presidents. Entering the city, the driver enters a grid of streets that inexorably lead to grand avenues that pass the National Mall's monuments and memorials and museums, not to mention the nation's halls of power. This is a city where marathon runners jog past the Jefferson and

Lincoln Memorials and the Washington Monument, around the White House and the Capitol. Visitors to the National Zoo take pictures of animals that may be gifts from a foreign government; drivers sit in traffic jams caused by motorcades for Russian presidents or English royalty. And hikers, crossing a bridge to a little island in the middle of the Potomac River, might stumble onto a network of semiwild hiking trails—presided over by a giant monument of Theodore Roosevelt. Even a mere hiking trail is caught up in the spectacle that is Washington, DC.

That spectacle, that history, is at the heart of the Potomac Heritage Trail, an existing and planned network of trails whose more than 800 miles provide insight into the history of America, the geography of the Eastern Seaboard, and the relationship between the two. In true Washington tradition, the Potomac Heritage Trail is all about who you know: that modest paved trail along the Potomac begins under the very shadow of George Washington's Mount Vernon. Connected to several presidents and a Supreme Court justice, segments of the trail date to the earliest days of the United States, when routes west—including a towpath along what are now the ruins of the Chesapeake & Ohio (C&O) Canal—linked the Potomac and Ohio River watersheds, part of a trade route that would ultimately stretch from Atlantic ports to the Gulf of Mexico.

Even earlier, during the French and Indian War, George Washington, then a young officer, traveled from the Eastern Seaboard to western Pennsylvania, approximately where Pittsburgh now sits at the confluence of the Monongahela, Allegheny, and Ohio Rivers. Washington's vision was that the Potomac River would one day connect the Chesapeake Bay with the Ohio River watershed. While his original project, the Patowmack Canal, did not succeed, it became a precursor of the C&O Canal. A trail sign might accurately say, "George Washington walked here."

The Potomac Heritage Trail is quintessentially Washingtonian in another way. It does not follow a straight line from here to there, but rather splinters into a network of competing and sometimes contradictory interests: history, military, nature, recreation. For long-distance hikers who have a strict point-A-to-point-B mentality, this trail is an anomaly, with spokes and loops, spurs, and parallels. Sometimes it runs on both sides of the Potomac River; sometimes road hiking is required to connect designated segments; sometimes the network includes a circular side trail.

Although the core of the trail is the line of travel that follows routes established to link the Chesapeake Bay to the Allegheny Highlands, this is not a route to thru-hike, eyes set on a far horizon, feet determinedly striding forth, mile after mile, with a goal in mind. Instead, it is a trail on which to meander, a trail to be explored, perhaps over a period of years. Side trails lead to places of historical and scenic interest. And each year sees more segments added to the trail.

Not only don't you have to stay on one trail going in one direction: you don't even have to be on foot. Much of the trail is open to cyclists and horseback riders as well as hikers. The majority of the trails in the network follow alongside river corridors, which were the original routes of transportation west. As a bonus, much of the Potomac River is navigable for kayakers and canoers—although not all of it is navigable for just anyone. The fierce rapids and falls at Great Falls, just upstream of Washington, DC, are a playground for Olympic kayakers, who need all of their skills to tackle the dangerous waters there. Flooding can cause difficult rapids elsewhere as well (check out the high-water marks at Harpers Ferry). Conversely,

PREVIOUS SPREAD: Lock 27, C&O Canal section of the PHT, Maryland

OPPOSITE: Lincoln Memorial and Washington Monument from across the Potomac River on the PHT, Washington, DC

BELOW: Great Falls, Potomac River, Maryland

in a low-water year, the upper Potomac may be only a few feet deep with places so shallow that it is difficult to float a boat.

The 800-plus-mile network of trails that make up the Potomac Heritage Trail feeds off a trunk line that connects the Chesapeake Bay, Washington, DC, and the Allegheny Plateau of Pennsylvania. The route passes through a mosaic of colonial settlements, birthplaces and homes of founding fathers, historic meeting points between Europeans and Native Americans, Civil War battlefields, sites of engineering marvels (including the great Paw Paw Tunnel), and some of America's first railroads. It's also a geography lesson, putting real landscapes to schoolbook terms like tidewater and piedmont, the sudden fall line at the Great Falls of the Potomac, the Blue Ridge near Harpers Ferry, and the Eastern Continental Divide (yes, there's a divide there, too).

WALKING INTO AMERICA

With its meandering nature and its starting location centered around the historically rich capital region, with a path that follows historic routes of trade and travel, and with a genesis that includes presidents from George Washington to Lyndon Johnson, it seems fair to say that the focus of the Potomac Heritage Trail is as much American history as it is recreation. So it makes sense to start a description of the trail not at the beginning, but somewhere in the middle—in Washington, DC—which is the spiritual, if not geographical, heart of the trail.

And if Washington is the heart of the trail, its backbone is the C&O Canal, which for nearly 100 years carried canal boats west through what was then a great, untrammeled wilderness, 184.5 miles to Cumberland, Maryland. The canal was built between 1828 and 1850. It operated sporadically (often stopped by floods) until 1924, when it ultimately died, a victim of the more efficient economics of railroading.

The canal was part of a network of transportation routes that were to open up trade with the great unknown west: from the mouth of the Chesapeake up the navigable Potomac to Washington, DC; from Washington by canal to Cumberland; from Cumberland overland to the Youghiogheny River; from the Youghiogheny to the Ohio River; from the Ohio down to the Mississippi (and perhaps back along the Natchez Trace Trail, another national scenic trail); and from there to points west.

OPPOSITE: C&O Canal Towpath beside Potomac River, Maryland

FOLLOWING SPREAD: The PHT along the C&O Canal Towpath, Maryland (top left); Burnside Bridge, Antietam National Battlefield, Maryland (bottom left); Harpers Ferry, West Virginia (right)

On a local level, the canal was a lifeline for Potomac River communities, enabling trade in coal, lumber, and agricultural products. For most of the canal, only remnants of the locks and ruins of lock-keepers' cottages are left. But in Georgetown, visitors can see something that looks a good bit like the canal of 100 years ago, and visit one of the interpretive centers along the route.

And not just canal and trade history lives along the trail. Engineering history was also made here with the construction of the 3,118-foot Paw Paw Tunnel (1836–1850), built to shorten a six-mile portion of the Potomac River that had five hairpin turns. Today, hikers walk through the tunnel—cool, damp smelling, and so long that only a pinprick of light indicates that there is an end with daylight on the other side.

Civil War history also abounds along the trail. Harpers Ferry, where John Brown launched his raid and lost his life, is a popular tourist day trip from Washington. Above Harpers Ferry in neighboring Bolivar Heights is the site of the Battle of Harpers Ferry, which marked the largest surrender of Union troops during the Civil War. Farther up the Potomac, a side trip from the trail can be made to Antietam, whose 22,000 dead make it the site of the bloodiest single day in United States history.

It's not only the places through which the trail passes that have a deep connection with American history: the trail itself has rubbed shoulders, so to speak, with historical figures. George Washington was only the first in a line of American leaders to be involved with a route along the Potomac. Lyndon Johnson was also connected with the trail, not just because he signed the National Trails System Act, but also because the view of the Potomac River was a favorite stopping point for him and for Lady Bird Johnson as they returned to the White House. Both are honored with parklands on the Potomac, the president at the Lyndon Johnson Memorial Grove and the first lady at Lady Bird Johnson Park.

Justice William O. Douglas of the United States Supreme Court, so famously associated with the mountains of his native Washington State and the wilderness along the Pacific Crest Trail that bears his name, was also involved with the C&O Canal as a recreation resource, long before there was a Potomac Heritage Trail, or indeed, even a National Trails System. In 1954, he traded his robes for hiking clothes, and organized an eight-day hike along the canal's towpath in an effort to save it from being converted to a parkway. That successful effort resulted in the canal becoming a national monument in 1971 and part of the newly authorized Potomac Heritage Trail in 1983.

THE ROUTE

From the Chesapeake Bay to Washington, DC, the Potomac Heritage Trail follows a combination of urban paths rich in history, paved bike paths, and multiuse paths. The evolving system of trails has sections on both sides of the Potomac, including bicycling routes on both sides of the wide estuary where the Potomac meets the Chesapeake Bay.

On the Virginia side of the Potomac River, local governments and trail volunteers are developing a continuous 100-mile footpath to connect Locust Shade Park in Prince William County with Whites Ferry near Leesburg. The 18-mile Mount Vernon Trail linking Mount Vernon, Alexandria, and Theodore Roosevelt Island is one part of the trail network; on the Washington side, the trail connects the Fort Circle Parks and dips into Rock Creek and Glover-Archbold Parks to create a top-notch urban hiking experience.

In Georgetown, the trail seems to finally make up its mind which way to go, and heads northwest on the 184.5-mile Chesapeake & Ohio Canal. This, the heart of the system, follows the north bank of the Potomac River to Cumberland, Maryland. Campsites are found every few miles, complete with water sources and garbage removal. Although the canal today is little more than a waterlogged ditch that provides habitat for turtles and frogs and a tangle of water-loving plants, the canal's towpath, with its flat, wide, obstruction-free footway, is a favorite of hikers, joggers, and bicyclists.

From Cumberland, the trail cuts away from its riparian corridor to pick up an overland route on the Great Allegheny Passage, a multiuse rail trail. Here, the route crosses the Eastern Continental Divide and leaves the Atlantic watershed. From here on, all waters will flow toward the Ohio, the Mississippi, and, ultimately, the Gulf of Mexico.

At Ohiopyle State Park, the Potomac Heritage Trail splits into two branches. Hikers can choose the scenic 70-mile Laurel Highlands Hiking Trail, which ends in Seward, Pennsylvania, or they can continue on the Great Allegheny Passage trail system and follow the historic trade route west along the Youghiogheny River to its confluence with the Monongahela River near Pittsburgh, forming the Ohio River.

FOLLOWING SPREAD: Potomac River from Point Lookout, Green Ridge State Forest, Maryland (left); Potomac River near Cumberland, Maryland (top right); the Western Maryland Scenic Railroad, which runs from Cumberland to Frostburg along the PHT (middle right); Keystone Viaduct near Meyersdale, Pennsylvania (bottom right)

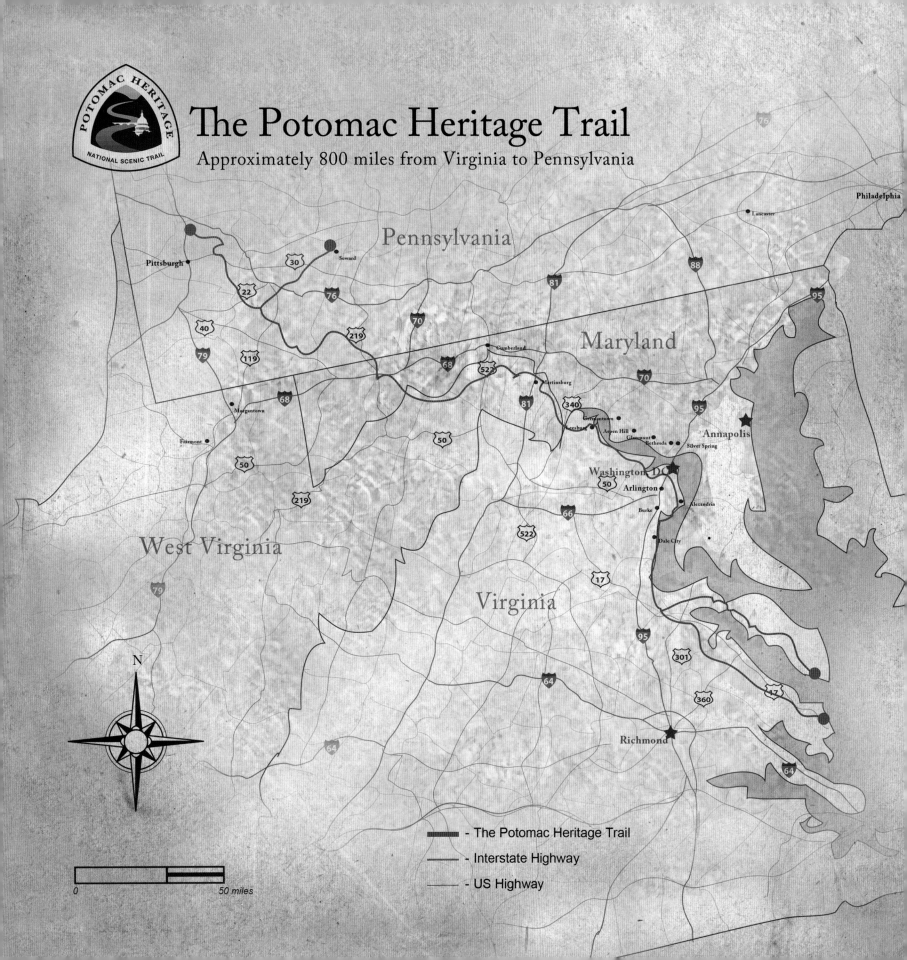

The Potomac Heritage Trail

Approximately 800 miles from Virginia to Pennsylvania

POTOMAC HERITAGE
NATIONAL SCENIC TRAIL

Philadelphia

Lancaster

Pennsylvania

Pittsburgh

Seward

30

22

76

40

219

79

119

68

Morgantown

Fairmont

50

219

West Virginia

79

Cumberland

68

522

81

Martinsburg

340

Germantown

Leesburg

Aspen Hill

Glenmont

Bethesda

Silver Spring

Maryland

70

95

Annapolis

Washington DC

50

Arlington

Burke

Alexandria

66

522

Dale City

17

95

301

360

95

64

Virginia

Richmond

64

17

64

N

- The Potomac Heritage Trail
- Interstate Highway
- US Highway

0   50 miles

PREVIOUS SPREAD: Blooming mountain laurel along the PHT, Pennsylvania (top left); chipmunk, Laurel Ridge section of the PHT, Pennsylvania (bottom left); the PHT through a rock maze, Pennsylvania (right)

OPPOSITE: Laurel Highlands section of the PHT near Beam Rocks, Pennsylvania

RIGHT: Shelter along Laurel Highlands section of the PHT (top); Ohiopyle Falls along the Youghiogheny River, Pennsylvania (bottom)

THE POTOMAC HERITAGE TRAIL

The Potomac Heritage Trail rewards visitors not only with sights on the trail itself, but also with nearby points of interest that offer a deeper look into American history. This makes the trail a route to be visited again and again, perhaps to explore Civil War sites or to experience the mid-Atlantic in all four seasons. The destinations below were selected to showcase the historic sites along and near the trail, as well as some of the scenic highlights.

MOUNT VERNON TRAIL (Virginia)

The paved, multiuse Mount Vernon Trail begins at George Washington's estate, and runs along the Virginia bank of the Potomac River 18 miles to Theodore Roosevelt Island. The Mount Vernon estate is one of the most popular tourist spots in the Washington area. Theodore Roosevelt Island contains a series of short hiking trails and a monument to Theodore Roosevelt, which, when one comes upon it tucked away in the forest, is every bit as imposing as any more famous monument on the National Mall. Cyclists doing the whole route in one day can stop for refreshments (and more historic sightseeing) in Alexandra, Virginia, or take a break at Gravelly Point Park, where planes landing at Reagan National Airport come right overhead.

GEORGETOWN VISITOR CENTER (Washington, DC)

The trendy and historic riverside district of Georgetown was founded in 1751—40 years before Washington, DC—on the site of what was once a Nacotchtank Native American village. This was the eastern terminus of the C&O Canal. During the summer months, the visitor center offers Georgetown walks every day at noon. Topics on these walks range from architecture to Civil War history.

GREAT FALLS TAVERN VISITOR CENTER (Maryland)

The site of impressive and dangerous rapids suitable for Olympic-level kayakers, Great Falls marks the change in elevation from the Atlantic coastal plain to the Piedmont. Visitors can take an hour-long trip back in time on a replica of an 1800s canal boat, led by a park ranger. The mule-drawn boat shows visitors a bit of the life of the canal men, passing along the old towpath and through a historic lock. Kids (or adults) can bring fruits or carrots to feed the mules. The boat usually operates from April until October; note that low water levels can affect the schedule.

PAW PAW TUNNEL (Maryland)

An engineering marvel for its time, the Paw Paw Tunnel can still be walked from one end to the other—with a flashlight in hand. Hikers can do an out-and-back in the tunnel, or can return via the two-mile-long Tunnel Hill Trail, whose interpretive markers describe the lives of the German and Irish workers who were part of the tunnel-building team. The name comes from the pawpaw trees along neighboring ridges.

HARPERS FERRY (West Virginia)

Across a pedestrian bridge located at the confluence of the Potomac and Shenandoah Rivers, the historic town of Harpers Ferry is an easy short detour from the Potomac Heritage Trail using a pedestrian bridge across the Potomac and crossing from Maryland to West Virginia. Steeped in its history—which is served up on the tourist-oriented main street with postcards, T-shirts, and Civil War museums—the Harpers Ferry National Historic Park makes a great jumping-off point for day hiking and boating explorations. The Potomac Heritage Trail here is briefly contiguous with the Appalachian Trail, which is headquartered in Harpers Ferry. Just south of the town, on the Maryland side of the river, the AT leaves the towpath to climb up to an excellent viewpoint at Weverton Cliffs, which offers unparalleled views of the rivers and the promontory where Harpers Ferry sits at their junction.

ANTIETAM (Maryland)

Antietam itself is not directly on the trail, but for visitors with cars, it's a short hop away and well worth the drive, especially since so much of the history on this route is bound up with the Civil War. Confederate and Union soldiers traded volleys up and down the river: the rebels took Harpers Ferry and the Yankees held on to Hancock upriver. Antietem puts the whole thing into perspective. Tours of the site of the Civil War's bloodiest day can be emotionally moving.

LAUREL HIGHLANDS HIKING TRAIL (Pennsylvania)

The 70-mile Laurel Highlands Hiking Trail, the main feature within Laurel Ridge State Park in western Pennsylvania, is one of two trail segments that lead to two different western termini for the Potomac Heritage Trail. Good accessibility to roads makes this ideal for day hikers starting in the northeast near Conemaugh Gorge or in Confluence (within Ohiopyle State Park)—or somewhere in the middle. In addition, there are shelters with tent pads and fresh water every eight to 10 miles.

OHIOPYLE TO CONFLUENCE ON THE GREAT ALLEGHENY PASSAGE (Pennsylvania)

This 10.5-mile river hike begins at Ohiopyle and ends at Confluence, where after a leg-stretching day hike, you'll find plenty of places for eating and resting. Spring (for the wildfowers) and autumn (for the foliage) are best. Summer is especially crowded on weekends. It's also a possible day trip for skilled and fit cross-country skiers or snowshoers. Ohiopyle State Park is also known for its dramatic Youghiogheny River Gorge, which claims some of the best white water in the eastern United States.

Top: Antietam National Battlefield; *Middle:* Mount Vernon, home of George Washington and southern terminus of the PHT; *Bottom:* C&O Canal reenactment boat ride in Georgetown

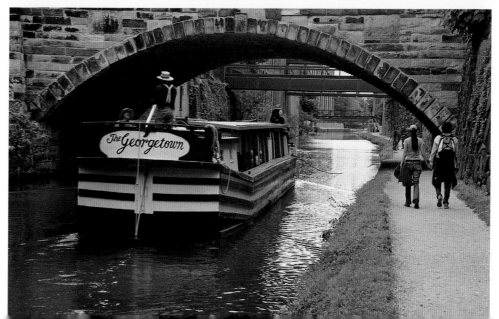

THE FLORIDA TRAIL

Forget dry feet. This trail has cypress swamps. Alligators. Hurricanes. Humidity. Subtropics. Monsoons. Manatees. Airboats. Water moccasins. Pelicans. Flamingos. Gum tree swamps. Salt marshes. Crystal-blue freshwater springs. • And then there are the place names: Alligator Alley. Big Cypress National Preserve. Billie Swamp Safari and Uncle Joe's Fish Camp. Lake Okeechobee. Juniper Springs. Green Swamp. Oh, and the Suwannee River. • Getting the idea yet? • The Florida Trail is a trail defined by water. The state has the longest coastline in the contiguous United States, and the trail that runs through it, first south to north, then east to west, stretches from Big Cypress National Preserve just north of the Everglades to Gulf Islands National Seashore just east of Pensacola, not far from the Alabama border. Almost all of the south–north route of the Florida Trail stays inland, away from the coast; the east–west section touches the Gulf of Mexico twice, but otherwise remains inland as well. But either way—fresh or salt, swamp or marsh—this is a trail about water.

To northerners, Florida, neatly pigeonholed as the nation's only subtropical state, is an undifferentiated collection of beaches and palm trees, high-rise condos and hurricanes. Even in the minds of nature lovers, pictures mingle in a sort of confused cornucopia of subtropical abundance: coral reefs and sea turtle hatcheries; rare ghost orchids and ubiquitous palmettos; and pelicans and alligators, the latter poking their noses out of cypress swamps draped with hanging epiphytes.

In reality, the Florida Trail encompasses more than 80 different habitats ranging from the white sand beaches of the Gulf of Mexico to cypress swamps, from freshwater springs to forests where hikers are as likely to see a bear as an alligator. True, trails like the Pacific Crest or the Continental Divide might boast more dramatic variety in terms of ecozones, running as they do from desert to alpine peak. And yes, ecologically, Florida is tethered by latitude and elevation to its subtropical environment. But within that constraint, there is a lush and fecund biodiversity here.

Culturally, too, the state offers surprising and sometimes extreme diversity (not to mention conflicted politics) with disparate land uses, communities, social mores, and religions colliding and enriching each other. Subcultures include Latinos—themselves representing a score or more traditions—Jewish retirees, Native Americans, local ranchers whose families date back generations, new arrivals who seek the good life in modern real-estate developments, and self-described Florida "crackers." As varied as the people are, Florida's icons also swing from the uninhibited family consumerism of Disney to the natural miracles of a Florida Keys coral reef, taking in Miami Beach, the Kennedy Space Center, the Everglades, the Daytona 500, and more. The Florida Trail winds its way through and among the development and the diversity, seeking backcountry in lands between shopping malls, suburbs, ranchlands, beaches, and the home of Mickey Mouse.

For out-of-state hikers, the Florida Trail is an entirely new ball game. The heat and the subtropical climate mean the luxury of warm-weather hiking—no snow to plan around, no extra layers of fleece or down jackets to haul in backpacks. Of course, these luxuries come with a price tag that experienced Florida hikers are well used to. And, it must be said, they can't resist the occasional temptation to play the gnarled old veteran to newcomers by being insouciant about the alligator that watches as you pitch your tent near its stream, or the mud that sucks the boots off your feet, or the water moccasin that is invisible on the trail until you almost step on it.

Perhaps the thing that is most different about the Florida Trail compared to the other national scenic trails is its elevation—or, rather, its lack of elevation change. Hikers become accustomed to feeling landscapes and ecosystems change with elevation gain and loss. On other trails, they hike uphill and notice that the composition of the forest changes, that spring comes later and fall comes earlier. On a mountain trail, a climb of 3,000 feet can take hikers from summer to winter. Not so in Florida, where the highest point in the entire state is a mere 345 feet above mean sea level. Yet on the Florida Trail, small differences in elevation gain or loss have huge ramifications, and a change of only a few feet, something completely inconsequential on other trails, can catapult hikers into an entirely new biological community. Five or six feet, sometimes less, is enough to make the difference between living wet and living dry, between hiking through swamps and sleeping on dry ground.

The lack of elevation change is also the reason that water pools just about everywhere. There often isn't any place lower for the water to run or drain, so rivers flow at a snail's pace toward the sea, unless diverted by channels designed to drain wetlands for use as agricultural land for sugarcane or grazing. In the wild areas, water collects in low points. When there is nowhere left for water to drain, and nowhere left for it to flow, it floods. Being a low point—a slight depression in an otherwise flat forest—the trail floods, too.

It is not, to put it mildly, a landscape immediately conducive to hiking, and until the 1960s there were relatively few places in the entire state for hikers to go.

STARTING A LONG-DISTANCE TRAIL

Indeed it could be said that, unlike the Appalachian Trail or the Pacific Crest Trail or even the Continental Divide Trail, whose lands have an abundance of hiking trails, the Florida Trail can trace its genesis to the lack of hiking trails in the state. A little more than 50 years ago, a Florida real-estate broker named Jim Kern wanted to take a hike. There being no obvious Florida hiking destination at the time—no trail

PREVIOUS SPREAD: Fern Hammock Springs, Juniper Prairie Wilderness, Ocala National Forest

OPPOSITE: The FT near its southern terminus, Big Cypress National Preserve

FOLLOWING SPREAD: The FT through Dwarf Pond Cypress, Big Cypress Preserve (left); the FT, Big Cypress National Preserve (right)

The Florida Trail

Approximately 1,400 miles from
Big Cypress National Preserve to Fort Pickens

- The Florida Trail
- Interstate Highway
- US Highway

FLORIDA TRAIL · NATIONAL SCENIC TRAIL

N

0   25 miles   50 miles   100 miles   150 miles   200 miles

Crest View
Niceville
Panama City   Callaway
Tallahassee
White Springs
Lake City
Jacksonville
Palm Valley
Middleburg
Saint Augustine
Gainesville
Ocala
Port Orange   Daytona Beach
New Smyrna Beach
Lady Lake
Orlando
Cocoa Beach
Kissimmee
New Port Richey
Satellite Beach
Tarpon Springs
Palm Bay
Clearwater
Tampa
Bartow
Saint Petersburg
Vero Beach
Palmetto
Sarasota
Port Saint Lucie
Venice
Punta Gorda
West Palm Beach
Fort Myers
Coral Springs
Naples   Fort Lauderdale
Miami
Homestead

organizations, no famous walking paths—he traveled clear up to the Appalachian Trail in North Carolina. Inexperienced in the ways of mountains, his vacation turned into what he later called a disaster.

But the small vacation left him with a big dream: Kern returned home determined to create hiking opportunities in a state where few existed. And "hiking opportunities" eventually came to mean a trail that spanned the entire state, south to north, then east to west. The Florida Trail Association, formed in 1966, collected dues of a dollar per member and went to work.

The early trail-building efforts of the Florida Trail ran along the lines of a now-familiar trail story: the combination of a trail visionary with a dream, a motivated community, and problems ranging from competing land uses to money. But every trail's particular issues are at least a little different, and Florida perhaps is more different than most. In addition to the normal growing pains, trail builders coped with getting lost in and bushwhacking through (or occasionally airboating into) undergrowth in which it would not be out of place to find an alligator, a bear, or a Florida panther. Much of the trail required completely new construction, as there were no old trails to revitalize. The challenges of extreme summer heat followed by hurricanes and flooding, coupled with a fecund environment in which trails could become overgrown in a single season, only added to the size of the task.

Still, in one sense, it was a fortuitous time to be thinking of starting a long-distance trail.

The need for infrastructure to develop trails and other types of outdoor recreation resources was clearly visible in the postwar boom in recreation participation. In a survey conducted in 1960 for the Outdoor Recreation Resources Review Commission, walking for pleasure ranked second among all recreation activities.

In February 1965, in his "Natural Beauty" message, President Lyndon Johnson called for the development and protection of a system of trails. The ideal, he said, would be a system that was balanced between creating trails near metropolitan areas, where he called for an abundance of trails for walking, cycling, and horseback riding, and remote backcountry, where he proposed copying the great Appalachian Trail. The system would be managed cooperatively with state government, local authorities, and private interests.

A mere three years later—certainly a short time, given the usual pace of government projects and the enormity of the proposal—the National Trails System Act of 1968 was passed. The Florida Trail—little more than an idea at the time—was not one of the original 14 trails slated for study, but volunteers took the idea as inspiration and in 1983 the Florida Trail was added to the National Scenic Trails System.

THRU-HIKING THE SUNSHINE STATE

The vast majority of trail usage on the Florida Trail—as with other national scenic trails—is by short-term hikers out for a day or a short backpack trip. Most of them are local trail enthusiasts: Florida may be one of the world's great tourist destinations, but the majority of tourists flock here not for the hiking trails but for the beaches, the golf courses, the diving, and, of course, the Mouse.

The exception is the thru-hikers, many of whom have previously done thru-hikes or very long stretches on other national scenic trails. One reason the Florida Trail appeals is that the best hiking season is during the winter, when most other long-distance trails are impassable. (Even the Natchez Trace Trail can occasionally have below-freezing temperatures, and the higher elevations of the Arizona Trail are impassable in winter.) As far as cold is concerned, in Florida, the only occasional frost is a "weather event."

Too, winter is when the water levels are lowest. The fall hurricane season is past, and though no one is promising dry feet—that would be a bit much to ask for—a winter start means many more dry stretches of trail, and shorter and shallower wet stretches. Time it right, and you may have only intermittent miles of ankle-deep wading; time it wrong, and you could be sloshing in muck up to your knees.

As with most other long-distance trails, the Florida Trail's route is not yet complete, so potential thru-hikers must seek out up-to-date information from recent guidebooks, recent thru-hikers, and the Florida Trail Association.

THE ROUTE

The Florida Trail is an end-to-end hike that, when completed, is expected to be about 1,400 miles in length, including a few loops and spurs that add to the system. Without these loops, the average thru-hiker today logs somewhere between 1,100 and 1,200 miles, depending on which loop segments they

PREVIOUS SPREAD: Alligator in Tamiami Canal near Oasis Visitor Center (top left); climbing aster in palmetto, Big Cypress National Preserve (middle left); Florida panther paw print on the FT, Big Cypress National Preserve (bottom left); the FT through Big Cypress Swamp, Big Cypress National Preserve (right)

FOLLOWING SPREAD: A thicket swamp from the nature trail at Billie Swamp Safari, Big Cypress Indian Reservation (left); melaleuca trees on the shore of Lake Okeechobee (top right); white ibis on the shore of Lake Okeechobee (bottom right)

choose and which roads and shortcuts they use to connect official trail segments.

Beginning in Big Cypress National Preserve, just north of the Everglades, the trail has a wet start through a primeval jungle of swamps and sawgrass prairies, black water and orchid-rich forests. This is a wild land of enormous ecological diversity, from bobcats to alligators to osprey to hawks to humming-birds to orchids. It's also one of the places that give the Florida Trail its reputation for swamp walking. The trail next passes through the Big Cypress Indian Reservation, settled by Seminoles who, in the early 1800s, refused the US government's "invitation" to move to Oklahoma. More than 100 years later, they did, however, accept the Florida Trail's request to pass through their land—the largest Native American reservation in Florida—although hikers must contact the tribe to obtain permission to hike there.

The next section of trail passes through the little-known Rotenberger Wildlife Management Area, a short section of old natural Florida that soon gives way to drained agricultural land south of Lake Okeechobee. The walk follows canals designed to drain the swamps and straighten out the rivers for cattle ranches and sugarcane fields. It's a view of old and new Florida, one after the other, compressed, with dramatic contrast.

Lake Okeechobee is the second-largest lake that is entirely within the borders of the United States, and the Florida Trail runs a 109-mile loop around it. Thru-hikers can choose either way, but there's an annual "Big O Hike" on the dike encircling the lake for those who want to do the whole thing in like-minded company. The shallow lake, usually no more than 13 feet deep, is framed by palm trees and lit by spectacular sunrises and sunsets.

From Okeechobee, the trail continues north-northwest, past the Avon Park Air Force Range and Prairie Lakes/Three Lakes Wildlife Management Area; then it splits into another, much longer, loop around Orlando. The west part of this loop goes to Kissimmee, whose eponymous river was an important thoroughfare for early Florida settlers. Oaks covered in resurrection ferns and Spanish moss–draped cypress show how anything can grow on anything in this rich ecological niche—and also attest to what can sometimes amount to more water than a hiker wants or needs. This section of the trail was developed with wildness in mind by Florida Trail planners concerned with the seemingly unchecked development to the east. The entire circle around Orlando is more than 350 miles.

The eastern corridor is the "main route," which passes through the Bull Creek Wildlife Management Area and the 300,000-acre Deseret Ranch, followed by a patchwork of state reserves, Native American lands, wetlands, and Orlando suburban roads and bike paths, before entering what many consider the jewel of the system: the Ocala National Forest.

It seems somehow fitting that the first Florida Trail blaze ever painted was in the Ocala National Forest. Just a short drive from the hustle of Disney World, this part of the trail is a microcosm of central Florida. It includes Florida's first wilderness and a series of clear-water springs, including the famous Juniper Springs, popular with scuba divers. Environments range from sand hills to hammocks, red-maple swamps to willow marshes, and grasslands to freshwater springs.

North of Ocala National Forest, the population density drops, the land becomes much more rural, and the trail becomes a patchwork, often on pleasant dirt roads through forests of scrub pines. The trail passes through Camp Blanding (a World War II prisoner-of-war camp that held captured Germans) and Mike Roess Gold Head Branch State Park, one of Florida's first state parks, then the Osceola National Forest and the Suwannee River.

By White Springs, the route finally turns west for real and heads firmly toward the Panhandle. It touches Gulf of Mexico waters at the St. Marks National Wildlife Refuge, the only national wildlife refuge where backpackers are allowed to camp, then heads a bit inland to pass south of Tallahassee, the state capital. In the Apalachicola National Forest, the trail's 80 miles go through forests and swamps and the Bradwell Bay Wilderness, Florida's second largest. The trail here is tough, with more swamp slogs and sometimes difficult navigation.

West of the Apalachicola National Forest, the trail returns to short alternating stretches of roads and trail, with noteworthy trail segments including those in Econfina Creek Water Management Area, St. Joe Timberlands, and Pine Log State Forest. The trail then loops around the north side of Eglin Air Force Base, and finally, fittingly, reaches the sea with a 28-mile beach walk on Santa Rosa Island, ending at Fort Pickens in Gulf Islands National Seashore.

OPPOSITE: Lotus flowers near Istokpoga Canal, Hickory Hammock Wildlife Management Area

FOLLOWING SPREAD: Aucilla River, Aucilla Conservation Area (left); the FT through a thicket of scrub oak, Ocala National Forest (top right); the FT through a cypress swamp, Osceola National Forest (bottom right)

PREVIOUS SPREAD: Great blue heron, St. Marks National Wildlife Refuge (top left); Monarch butterflies, St. Marks National Wildlife Refuge (middle left); alligator, St. Marks National Wildlife Refuge (bottom left); Aucilla River, Aucilla Wildlife Management Area (right)

LEFT: Sawgrass and tree islands in Marsh Point, St. Marks National Wildlife Refuge (top); the FT near Elgin Air Force Base (bottom)

OPPOSITE: Naval Live Oaks Reservation

FOLLOWING SPREAD: Sea oats and grasses in dunes, Gulf Islands National Seashore (left); interior cabin chamber at Fort Pickens, Gulf Islands National Seashore (top right); the northern terminus of the FT, Fort Pickens, Gulf Islands National Seashore (bottom right)

THE FLORIDA TRAIL

These Florida Trail highlights were contributed by Florida Trail expert Sandra Friend, author of *Along the Florida Trail* (with photos by Bart Smith), and coauthor, along with John Keatley, of *The Florida Trail Guide.*

BIG CYPRESS SWAMP

The Florida Trail begins in one of America's most unusual habitats, a river more than 40 miles wide and a few inches to a few feet deep. Entirely fed by rainfall, the Big Cypress Swamp is inundated by a sheet flow of crystal-clear water that moves slowly toward the Gulf of Mexico, nourishing sawgrass prairies and cypress strands. This southernmost section of the Florida Trail is a tough place for backpackers, since wading—and soggy camping on small islands—is guaranteed for three days between the trail's southern terminus at Oasis Ranger Station and higher ground north of Interstate 75.

LAKE OKEECHOBEE

Circling the second-largest freshwater lake entirely within the United States, the Florida Trail loops Lake Okeechobee atop a man-made structure, the Herbert Hoover Dike, established in the 1930s for flood control. The dike makes it impossible for the lake to be seen from surrounding roads. Only those who walk along it enjoy the immense panoramas, with resplendent sunrises and sunsets, on this inland sea of 730 square miles.

BARGE CANAL DIGGINGS, CROSS FLORIDA GREENWAY

Switchbacks, steep drops, and eroding hillsides aren't what you'd expect in this part of central Florida, but a long-abandoned attempt at building a canal that would slice Florida in two left man-made mounds of earth that the forests reclaimed, and the Florida Trail traverses between the Land Bridge and Pruitt trailheads, flanking Interstate 75 south of the city of Ocala.

OCALA NATIONAL FOREST

Home to the largest contiguous sand pine scrub forest in the world, the Ocala National Forest is where the Florida Trail first began being built in 1966. Today, it's by far the most popular destination along the trail. With nearly 70 unbroken miles of footpath through rolling hills topped with longleaf pine, open prairies, and diminutive scrub forests, it features side trails to first-magnitude springs forming oases between ancient dunes.

LITTLE-BIG ECON STATE FOREST

As the Florida Trail follows the bluffs above the Econlockhatchee River, it dips through the shade of ancient live oaks and dense thickets of cabbage palms, and crosses palmetto prairies and bog bridges over clusters of carnivorous pitcher plants. The press of suburbia northeast of Orlando is just beyond the forest's boundaries, but it rarely intrudes.

RICE CREEK SANCTUARY

Developed as a rice and indigo plantation by British loyalists, the swamps surrounding Rice Creek are laced with levees that keep the trails above the wetlands. Ancient cypress forms the canopy above, with towering trees adding to the primordial feel. Florida's seventh-largest cypress is along this section of the trail, as well as one of the finer shelters available to backpackers.

SUWANNEE RIVER

Following the fabled Suwannee River for nearly 80 miles, the Suwannee section of the Florida Trail features rugged terrain with fascinating geology. Deep sinkholes, bubbling springs, natural bridges, and limestone flowerpot formations can be seen from the trail as hikers scramble in and out of side channels carved by the river during its flood stages. Several waterfalls cascade toward the river, which offers white sandy beaches for camping when water

levels are low. Given the floodplain nature of the river, which drains the Okefenokee Swamp in Georgia, timing a trek along the Suwannee can be a challenge in rainy seasons.

AUCILLA SINKS

The Florida Trail at its most primeval, the Aucilla Sinks section leads hikers through a jagged landscape of limestone karst where archaeological excavations have found evidence of human habitation in the Pleistocene Era. The river plays peekaboo in caves, sinks, and solution holes, running beneath the earth's surface before emerging again to flow toward the Gulf of Mexico.

RED ROCKS BLUFFS, BLACKWATER RIVER STATE FOREST

Atop high bluffs above the sinuous form of Juniper Creek, the Florida Trail puts on its best panorama. Topped with the bright-pink blooms of mountain laurel each spring, these crumbling clay-and-sand promontories offer an eagle's-eye view of a scene that doesn't feel like Florida, but is.

UWF DUNES PRESERVE

Along the seashore section of the Florida Trail, not far from its northern terminus at Fort Pickens, the footpath scrambles up and down over tall dunes providing panoramas of both the Gulf of Mexico and Santa Rosa Sound. Delicate coastal scrub fringes the high points along the sound, where a backpacker's campsite comes with a sea breeze.

Top: The FT through Big Cypress National Preserve; *Middle Left:* Sandhill cranes along shore of Rodman Reservoir, Ocala National Forest; *Middle Right:* The FT through Rice Creek Sanctuary; *Bottom:* Little Shoals rapids along Suwannee River

THE NATCHEZ TRACE TRAIL

The difficulty of putting sprawling ideas like trails into neat government categories is that sometimes the categories don't quite fit. Nowhere is that more true than in the case of the Natchez Trace Trail. • All the other national scenic trails are continuous footpaths—although they may also include spurs, loops, and trail networks. And while rules about motorized and multiple-recreation use are not consistent throughout the system, on other national scenic trails nonmotorized travel is almost always a priority. The Appalachian Trail is most restrictive, with no motorized or cycling use permitted anywhere, and equestrians permitted only on the few sections where horse use predated the trail's location. The Pacific Crest Trail permits equestrians and is graded for stock use—riding clubs are active maintainers on some sections—but motorized vehicles and bicycles are forbidden. On other trails, rules vary by district and land-management agency: snowmobiles, jeeps,

ATVs, and dirt bikes are allowed on some sections of many trails. But throughout the system, hiking is somehow paramount.

The Natchez Trace Trail is almost the exact opposite: its backbone is not a footpath, but a scenic parkway. The trail segments designed for walkers, cyclists, and horseback riders are occasional offshoots and spurs, clearly secondary. The Natchez Trace Trail was never envisioned to be a long, continuous footpath; currently, only about 60 miles of trail, out of the parkway's 444 miles, have been developed for hiking and horseback riding. Walkers and cyclists may use the shoulder of the parkway, but the parkway is no more a hiking trail than an RV campground is a backcountry campsite.

The Natchez Trace Trail follows the route of the historic Natchez Trace, a Native American travel route that became the backbone of trade to the lower Mississippi. In 1968, it was one of the 14 routes named in the original National Trails System Act as a candidate for possible inclusion in the new system. In 1978, the act was updated, and a new type of trail was added to the system: national historic trails. With its continuous paved roadway, its emphasis on historic sites, and its lack of a designated continuous footway, the Natchez Trace Trail seems more suited to this newer designation. Instead, it lost its way in the thickets and briars of the National Scenic Trails System and became a national scenic trail.

It seems ironic, then, that the Natchez Trace might be called the nation's first recognized long-distance walking route. Dating back thousands of years, it began as a trail for bison and migrating ungulates, and was first used by Native Americans following game between the uplands of what is now Tennessee and the lower Mississippi River near the Gulf of Mexico. In the 18th century, the Trace—then only a collection of meandering paths all headed in the same direction—was used by explorers, traders, post riders, and the military, until it became an established route. So-called "Kaintuck" boatmen would ferry trading goods down the Cumberland, Tennessee, and Mississippi Rivers, drop their cargo at the port of Natchez, and walk back home. And then they would turn back around and do it all over again. Carrying everything they needed on their backs—or hoping to find supplies en route—these traders, who made the trip not once but multiple times, can be considered some of the nation's first long-distance hikers.

PREVIOUS SPREAD: Owl Creek Mounds, Tombigbee National Forest, Mississippi

OPPOSITE: Casino boat on Mississippi River near Natchez Under-the-Hill, Mississippi

FOLLOWING SPREAD: Grand Village, Natchez State Park, Mississippi (left); Sunken Trace, a deeply eroded section of the Old Trace, Mississippi (top right); Owens Creek Waterfall, Mississippi (bottom right)

The National Trails System Act was intended to meet a broad spectrum of recreational needs, and each trail, it seems, fills the goals of the National Scenic Trails System slightly differently. The Natchez Trace's history as a millennia-old footpath makes it arguably an interesting, if unusual, national scenic trail, as well as a recreational resource with diverse opportunities. With a continuous route along and parallel to the Old Trace, the entire corridor of the Natchez Trace Trail is a unit of the National Park Service, with a brief break around Jackson, Mississippi. On the Natchez Trace Trail, the idea of walking in the footsteps of history is quite literal. With its 444-mile parkway for scenic driving; with its bicycling, horseback riding, and hiking opportunities; and with its interpretive centers, campgrounds, and picnic areas, the Natchez Trace Trail achieved national scenic trail status in 1983.

HUNTING THEN TRADING; NOW HIKING

Almost like a James Michener novel, the story of the Natchez Trace begins long before the dawn of human history, in this case with the herds of bison that once traveled between salt licks in western Tennessee near present-day Nashville and the alluvial grasslands along the lower Mississippi River. The animals avoided steep terrain as they moved between ridges and valleys, creating a path that made foot-sense for humans as well as game. When Native Americans came on the scene, their hunters followed the paths or "traces" of the herds until the route became a relatively well-worn human path, complete with communities. Evidence of these early settlements includes the 2,000-year-old Pharr Mounds, a Native American site located near Tupelo, Mississippi. Just west of the Trace and north of Highway 61 near Natchez, the eight-acre Emerald Mound is the second-largest Native American ceremonial mound in the United States, and is a designated national historic site.

The Natchez Trace continued to offer a viable route of travel when Europeans arrived; Spanish explorers may have used it as early as the 17th century. The first European explorers depended on Choctaw and Chickasaw guides, whose people had been using the Trace for generations. In the 18th century, under an agreement with Native Americans, European settlers widened the footpath so that it could be used by horses and wagons. President Thomas Jefferson envisioned the Trace as a postal route to connect the end of Daniel Boone's Wilderness Road in Nashville with the Mississippi River and, from there, with settlements along the Gulf Coast.

Meanwhile, traders were using the Trace in whatever condition they found it. On the downstream part of their journey, floating from Nashville to Natchez, they rode on flatboats stuffed with trading goods from the upper and lower Ohio, Tennessee, and Cumberland River Valleys. This, however, was a one-way proposition: unable to float their boats back upstream, the boatmen would sell their goods, including the wood from their flatboats, and hike back via the Trace. And for those who think today's long-distance hiking trails are crowded, consider this: by 1810, more than 10,000 barge runners and traders might be coursing back and forth along the rivers and the Trace in a single year.

The traffic brought services to the boondocks: about 50 so-called stands—collections of inns and trading posts run by both whites and Native

OPPOSITE: A section of the Old Trace along the Natchez Trace Parkway, Mississippi

BELOW: Rural scene near Magnum Mound, Mississippi

The Natchez Trace Trail

Approximately 444 miles from Tennessee to Mississippi

NATCHEZ TRACE
NATIONAL SCENIC TRAIL

Tennessee

Mississippi

Alabama

- Clarksville
- Nashville
- Jackson
- Memphis
- Corinth
- Oxford
- Tupelo
- Starkville
- Huntsville
- Decatur
- Chattanooga
- Birmingham
- Tuscaloosa
- Montgomery
- Jackson
- Laurel
- Natchez
- Mobile

- The Natchez Trace Trail
- Interstate Highway
- US Highway

N

0   50 miles

Americans—were established along the route, among them Washington, Mississippi (the old state capital); Port Gibson (once a prosperous mansion-lined town and, more recently, an important boycott site in the Civil Rights movement); and "old" Greenville (where Andrew Jackson did business as a slave trader). Settlers, schools, churches, and itinerant preachers quickly followed: Baptists, Methodists, Presbyterians, and more, aiming to convert Native Americans and save the souls of the roughnecks along the trail.

Given the crime statistics, they weren't entirely successful: Natchez's Under-the-Hill district—the port and riverfront section that sat under the bluffs where the solid citizens lived—was a rowdy area of whorehouses, gambling houses, and bars where traders let off steam and lightened their money-loaded pockets before heading back home on foot. Although these "Kaintucks" were as tough as the life they led, the temptation those cash-filled pockets posed to outlaws and brigands was irresistible: the Natchez Trace became host to some of America's first organized crime gangs, which operated for years from hideouts along the route.

Perhaps the Trace's most famous victim was Meriwether Lewis, of Lewis and Clark fame, then a mere 35 years old. He died in Grinder's Stand near today's Hohenwald, Tennessee, reportedly of two gunshot wounds. *Two*. An inquiry returned a finding of suicide, which was accepted by both President Thomas Jefferson and William Clark, Lewis's partner. But Lewis's family was convinced that the innkeeper at Grinder's Stand somehow was involved in the death.

By 1830, technology and settlement patterns doomed the Natchez Trace to temporary, as it turned out, obscurity. Unused sections of the old path were consumed by the fecund vegetation; the parts that remained in passable condition were used only for local transport and trade between rural communities. The big-ticket trans-America trade moved to Mississippi River steamboats, now capable of battling the current and traveling in both directions. Adding insult to injury, Jackson's Military Road, built in 1820, offered a shorter land alternative. The arduous and dangerous walk on the Trace, now impractical, became obsolete.

A hundred years later, the fortunes of the Trace changed yet again. An Emergency Appropriation Act of June 19, 1934, allocated initial funds for the construction of a scenic parkway to follow the approximate route of the Old Trace, to be undertaken by the Civilian Conservation Corps, one of scores of make-work Depression projects that built roads and trails and iconic "parkitecture" lodges in America's national parks and forests. Constructed by skilled artisans, many of these projects are still admired and in use today. The Natchez Trace was given national park status in 1938. Today, it encompasses a 444-mile two-lane road and 45,000 acres of parkland stretching through parts of three states.

THE ROUTE

Today's Natchez Trace Parkway, containing the parkway, adjacent lands, historic sites, and surviving stretches of the Old Trace, some of which are part of the Natchez Trace Trail, is a unit of the National Park System. The two-lane road is closed to commercial traffic and has a speed limit of 50 miles per hour. The general contour of the route is a northeast-to-southwest line between Nashville, Tennessee, and Natchez, Mississippi, en route crossing a small section of northwest Alabama, and passing through Jackson and Tupelo, Mississippi. While the parkway follows the approximate route of the Old Trace, it does not follow the original path exactly, engineering demands for a highway being somewhat different than the whims of the animal herds that first established the route. Nonetheless, parts of the highway use the Old Trace, and other sections of the original path are accessible from the highway, some of them as marked hiking trails. Often, the combination of soft compressible earth and centuries of erosion has caused the Old Trace to seemingly sink into the earth, surrounded on both sides by high, vegetation-covered banks. Following it takes the modern-day hiker into a world that might well look familiar to those who walked here a hundred years ago.

Visitors identify their position on the parkway by means of mile markers, starting at 0 (at Natchez) and ending at 444 (near Nashville). Because the Natchez Trace was heavily used by settlers only for a short time, cities were only sparsely developed along the route: in addition to Nashville and Natchez at the termini, the only population centers on the route are Jackson (the capital of Mississippi) and Tupelo (best known as the birthplace of Elvis Presley). As a result of its largely rural character, plus its protection as part of the National Park System, the Natchez Trace Trail remains relatively undeveloped.

PREVIOUS SPREAD: Pharr Mounds, Mississippi (top left); cypress trees near Tennessee-Tombigbee Waterway, Mississippi (bottom left); wisteria blooming along the Natchez Trace Trail near Tupelo, Mississippi (right)

FOLLOWING SPREAD: Beaver dam across Rock Spring, Alabama (top left); stepping blocks crossing Colbert Creek along Rock Spring Nature Trail, Alabama (bottom left); fisherman wading across Metal Ford, Buffalo River, Tennessee (right)

OPPOSITE: Balanced rocks, Glenrock Branch, Tennessee

RIGHT: Rural Tennessee countryside from Baker Bluff Overlook (top); blooming redbud near the northern terminus of the Natchez Trace Trail, Tennessee (bottom)

THE NATCHEZ TRACE TRAIL

The park maintains a series of historic sites on and near the Natchez Trace, along with campgrounds and hiking, cycling, and equestrian trails spread throughout the length of the parkway. In addition, the nearby towns are worth the short detours. They show different facets of Mississippi history, from the great antebellum mansions of Natchez to sites from the Civil Rights movement in Jackson and Port Gibson to Elvis's birthplace in Tupelo.

EMERALD MOUND (Mississippi)
The second-largest Native American temple mound in the United States was built and used between 1300 and 1600 CE by the forerunners of the Natchez Indians. Using a natural hill as a base, they reshaped the land into a great artificial plateau 770 feet long, 435 feet wide, and 35 feet high by trimming the top and filling the sides. This site is located at milepost 10.3.

ROCKY SPRINGS (Mississippi)
Nestled between the Natchez Trace Parkway and the Old Port Gibson Road is the ghost town of Rocky Springs, which thrived in the late 19th century. Today, the old Rocky Springs Methodist Church, the cemetery, and several building sites still exist and are accessible from the parkway. This site is located at milepost 54.8.

CYPRESS SWAMP (Mississippi)
A boardwalk leads through a cypress swamp, where visitors can see a unique ecosystem of water tupelo and bald cypress trees, which can live in deep water for long periods. This site is located at milepost 122.0.

BYNUM MOUNDS (Mississippi)
The Bynum Mounds site attests to the Natchez Trace's history as a trade route long before European settlers came to town: artifacts found there include flint from Ohio, greenstone from the Alabama-Tennessee piedmont region, and seashells from the Gulf Coast. Other Trace artifacts, some of which can be seen at the Parkway Visitors Center near Tupelo, include scrapers, earthenware pots, fabrics, and cord. This site is located at milepost 232.4.

TUPELO VISITOR CENTER (Mississippi)
The history of the modern Natchez Trace Parkway and the ancient Trace is summarized at the Natchez Trace Parkway Visitor Center in Tupelo, Mississippi, right on the Trace. There's an information center, bookstore, exhibits, and restrooms. Outside, there is a short nature walk. A hiking trail leads to the Chickasaw Village Site (milepost 261.8), which once contained a few houses and a fort. In the nearby city of Tupelo, visitors can tour Elvis's birthplace and check out the hardware store where he bought his first guitar. This site is located at milepost 266.0.

PHARR MOUNDS (Mississippi)
Northern Mississippi's largest archaeological site contains eight dome-shaped burial mounds. The 90-acre site was used as a burial site between 100 and 1200 CE by nomadic Native American hunters and gatherers. This site is located at milepost 286.7.

MERIWETHER LEWIS SITE (Tennessee)
The commander of the Lewis and Clark expedition is memorialized here. He died at the Grinder House, whose ruins are a scant 230 yards away. The Grinder House contains exhibits depicting the history of the Natchez Trace. The Meriwether Lewis site includes a campground, pioneer cemetery, picnic tables, restrooms, hiking trails, and a section of the Old Trace. This site is located at milepost 385.9.

TOBACCO FARM (Tennessee)
On this typical tobacco farm, circa early 1900s, a 10-minute loop trail circles through tobacco fields to the barn, where tobacco is hanging to dry. A narrow two-mile section of the Old Trace with sweeping valley views leads from the farm to the parkway. This site is located at milepost 401.4.

Top Left: Alligators resting in cypress swamp; *Bottom Left:* Meriwether Lewis memorial at Grinder's Stand; *Top Right:* A ceremonial mound atop Emerald Mound; *Middle Right:* A water well, a remnant of the ghost town of Rocky Springs; *Bottom Right:* Chickasaw Village Site

THE ARIZONA TRAIL

➤ IT'S A DRY HEAT ◄

In the Superstition Mountains, on a scorched trail far away from the main traffic paths of hikers or horsemen, there is a spot where little rock piles known as cairns mark the route. Even so, it's not entirely clear where a hiker is supposed to go. One choice is to follow the cairns, which lead, like breadcrumbs, down a chute that requires a drop of some six feet onto a rocky ledge. Beyond that, one cannot see. Another choice is to follow a much friendlier looking path, which contours around the canyon in a logical sort of way—though it might have been made by bighorn sheep or deer. The gentle path versus the improbable drop: Can this possibly be the right route? What if you go down— and get stuck on that ledge? And what if you can't climb back up? • If you have read Edward Abbey's *Desert Solitaire*, you will have a good idea of the possibilities: the casual drop down the rock, the sudden realization that you cannot go farther forward because of the even steeper drop ahead, the gradual, dawning panic as you realize that you also cannot climb back up what had been so easy to jump down. Shadows shorten as a blazing sun inexorably marches across the sky. Temperatures rise, and you realize your life span is measured in drops of water, specifically the so very finite number of drops remaining in your canteen. Indeed, if you have read *Desert Solitaire*, you might not go down that ledge at all—not without a hiking partner to stay behind and go for help if needed, not without a rope, not without fear. Edward Abbey managed to scramble out of his canyon, hauling himself by the grace of a piece of vegetation that amazingly held his weight. Would you be so lucky?

Heat and sun and a nagging concern about water: these are the constant companions of the Arizona Trail, a trek of stark and startling beauty, of fierce and merciless nature, where water and heat are the only things that matter, one the giver of life, the other its destroyer.

Yet it is also a trail of remarkable diversity, with saguaro-covered hills in the south of the state, manzanita shrubs, pine forests, sky-island mountains, bird-attracting riparian areas, famed red-rock formations near Sedona, and endless views everywhere. Mile for mile, the Arizona Trail offers a range of ecosystems that is among the most diverse in the National Trails System. Day hikers can experience Mexican plains or Colorado peaks only a few miles from a trailhead parking lot. And thru-hikers can trek across nearly a continent's worth of diversity in a single state.

Diverse as the experiences are, a common thread runs through them: water, or rather, the lack of water. Arizona is the fourth driest state in the United States with an average mean rainfall of just under 13.7 inches a year, and this fact underlies the experience of backpacking on the Arizona Trail. The lack of frequent natural water sources requires day hikers to bring enough water for the planned trip and to turn back when canteens start to run low. For backpackers, who depend on springs, streams, and water-storage tanks for camping, the Arizona Trail is single-mindedly and above all a quest for water. Every decision a backpacker makes, every campsite, every rest spot, every meal is about water: do you have enough, and where can you get more?

Stock tanks, ephemeral streams, an occasional spring: these are the beacons of an Arizona Trail hiker's route. There is nowhere on the trail where backpackers can blithely hike past a running spring without filling up and checking maps and guidebooks to learn how much to carry until the next water might be found. When backpackers find water, they drink more than they think they can. They walk with the knowledge of precisely how much water they have left in their canteens; they watch the level go down like misers, knowing that enough is never enough; they calculate miles per liter. They know—they *must* know—where the next spring is, and the one after that.

Being this close to the necessities of life, to the fundamental needs of an animal in a dry place, is for many hikers one of the attractions of the Arizona Trail. It is a trail where communing with nature happens in a very real and physical way. The resulting experience is a connection with the land that is unique among the national scenic trails. So hikers check the maps, they look for old ruined cabins (almost always built near some kind of water source), they feel for water in the cool dark sand under rocks in steep draws, they notice signs of animal life. And they learn that many things can look like water when there is no water to be found: Shadows in a dry draw look like water. Dead leaves on the trail look like water. Piles of pebbles look like water. Dark sand looks like water. The shiny skin of a manzanita looks like water. They look for green even though the color green can be deceptive; it can mean cottonwoods or creosote. Only one points the way to water.

Sometimes, the best thing to do is simply copy the animals that have learned to live here—staying out of the heat of the day and conserving moisture by wearing sun protection. (Yes, desert plants and animals invented sunscreen. They use secretions, saliva, dirt, or wax as skin guards.) And always, always, drinking.

Dryland hiking is not a unique challenge for long-distance hikers: the Continental Divide and Pacific Crest Trails both cross hundreds of miles of desert, semidesert, drylands, and scrub. For hikers on any of these trails, the definition—is it desert? arid lands? scrub?—is less important than the reality of the equation: water equals life, simple as that.

Hikers may feel a little bit envious of the cacti, which have the whole thing so well worked out.

A GRASSROOTS SUCCESS STORY

The Arizona Trail is one of the newer national scenic trails. Like virtually all the other national scenic trails, it traces its history back to one advocate—a familiar story by now. On the Arizona Trail, it was

Flagstaff history teacher and hiking enthusiast Dale Shewalter, who, in the 1970s, envisioned a border-to-border trail to connect communities with natural features like mountains, canyons, deserts, and forests, as well as public lands, historic sites, various trail systems, and wilderness areas. In 1985, Shewalter walked across the state to scout a route and prove it could be done. Shortly after, he began publicizing his idea to trail users and land managers. Work began in the late 1980s. In the 1990s, the Arizona State Parks assumed the leadership role in coordinating the trail; the Arizona Trail Association was formed as a non-profit in 1994. With support across land-management agencies, and a grassroots campaign that attracted a variety of trail users and local stakeholders, work progressed quickly and effectively. The trail was added to the National Scenic Trails System in 2009.

About 70 percent of the trail passes through Forest Service land, and another 15 percent through National Park Service and Bureau of Land Management land. But trail organizers are quick to point out that this is not just a federal government effort, which may be one of the secrets of its success. According to Eric Smith, who was trail steward during the critical trail-building years between 1994 and 1996, much of the trail's success is attributable to a long list of donors, participants, and volunteers from both the private and public sector.

MORE THAN JUST DESERTS

Arizona's average 13.7 inches of rainfall is just that: an average. Although the south-central section of the trail spends significant mileage in regions that get fewer than 10 inches of rain a year, much of the rest of the trail has dramatic changes in elevation, latitude, and rainfall, creating much more than a simple desert hike. On the watery side of the 13.7-inch average are mountainous sections with enough snow to house a few ski areas, one of which is just 120 miles north of the trail's southern terminus near the Mexican border. In the San Francisco Peaks near Flagstaff, it might snow in June.

The trail starts in the sky-island country of the Huachuca Mountains at the Coronado National Memorial. The ecological metaphor of sky islands is a virtual guarantee of biological diversity. In this kind of ecological system, hot and dry desertlike expanses of land replace ocean waters, mountains in the sky replace islands in the sea. As with maritime islands,

sky islands are isolated from each other, providing homes to species that cannot survive for long in the surrounding environment—in one case, the sea, in the other case, the dry valley floors. Thus isolated from one another, individual populations might develop their own adaptations; in time, as in the Galápagos Islands, they can become their own species.

So, from the memorial to Coronado, hikers start with a climb from which they can look down into the plains that spread south into Mexico. The dun browns of the valley floors are interrupted by occasional dramatically craggy peaks. Arizonans are fond of pointing out that their state contains six of the seven climate zones in North America, and hikers might experience several of them in a single day.

Indeed, as the Arizona Trail climbs and slides throughout the state's jagged and abrupt mountains, it takes hikers on the ecological equivalent of a roller-coaster ride: up to the ponderosas, down to the piñons, up to the oaks, down to the saguaros. In 800 miles, thru-hikers do the ecological (if not the mileage) equivalent of walking from Mexico to Canada. The trail passes near the summit of Humphreys Peak, the state's 12,637-foot high point, where snow may linger well into summer. Two weeks later, hikers may encounter temperatures of 100 degrees or more in the guts of the Grand Canyon. And a mere day later—still in summer—up at the North Rim, temperatures may plummet to 40 degrees or even colder.

Adding to the diversity are the riparian corridors, which in drylands attract endemic birds, plus migrating birds that depend on the few relatively well-watered sections along their routes. In addition to avian rarities such as the elegant trogon, whiskered screech owl, blue-throated and white-eared hummingbirds, sulphur-bellied and buff-breasted flycatchers, and red-faced warbler, the Arizona Trail hiker who is both lucky and observant might see mountain lions, bighorn sheep, coyotes, javelinas, elk, and antelope.

In the lowlands, fierce conditions (like ground temperatures that can exceed 160 degrees Fahrenheit in summer) create even more variations and astonishing adaptations that enable plants and animals to survive. Prickly pear cacti are ubiquitous, with their yellow blooms and protective needles. Fuzzy soft-looking teddy-bear cholla attack passersby with a vengeance, sometimes by breaking off and attaching their thorns to clothing and skin. Agave, which

OPPOSITE: View toward Rincon Valley from the Manning Camp Trail section of the Arizona Trail, Saguaro National Park

FOLLOWING SPREAD: View from Romero Pass along the shoulder of Mount Lemmon, Pusch Ridge Wilderness, Santa Catalina Mountains (left); cholla near Antelope Peak (top right); osprey nest in saguaro cactus near Antelope Peak (bottom right)

flower only once in their lives and then topple over and die, sprout ridiculous stalks that look like plants in a Dr. Seuss book. Giant water-hoarding saguaros look like an army of cheerful Gumbies crowned with hats of surprisingly delicate white flowers that bloom only at night when the sun and heat can't leach away their water. And the dreaded catclaw acacia grab and hold hikers, earning their nickname as the "wait a minute" bush.

Evil? Misanthropic? No, merely adaptive. On cacti, for instance, thorns are remnant leaves that protect the plant's store of internal moisture from water-seeking animals and also reflect light away from the plant. In lieu of leaves, many cacti and trees use their green skin to conduct the photosynthetic process. The thick, waxy skin of the cactus prevents evaporation.

As for the animals, unfortunately some of their more xerocolic adaptations can't be copied by mere humans. The kangaroo rat, for example, is a tiny rodent so well adapted that it extracts all the water it needs from its food (primarily dried seeds and grasses) and can go its entire life without drinking water at all. The mule deer, with its thick, hard lips, is capable of chewing on cactus thorns.

Humans can only admire these hardy denizens—for themselves, they must resort to modern gear. So they bring extra water bags, of course, and maps or a GPS to help find the water with which to fill them. They wear breathable, light-colored, SPF-rated clothing to prevent evaporation and sunburn, sunshading hats, and bandannas, and some hikers even use parasols.

And sometimes, avoidance is the most sensible course: just as the tops of Colorado's 14ers are off-limits to all but the most experienced climbers in winter, part of the Arizona Trail is most sensibly avoided during the hottest months. There is a reason why desert animals are not out and about at noon on a sunny July afternoon. Hiking the lower elevations of the Arizona Trail in the summer is a fool's mission—and in some sections of the trail, frankly dangerous. It is far better to deal with the occasional snows of January. Most, although not all, sections of the trail are passable in winter. Prime hiking seasons are spring and fall, when temperatures are moderate. In spring, seasonal water sources are most likely to be flowing.

More than anything, the Arizona Trail is a trail of contrasts. For day hikers, it offers almost unlimited opportunities to see and experience an astonishing variety of ecosystems, sometimes within a single hike. In spring and fall, temperatures are mostly mild, the chance of rain is slight, and the wide-open country promises plenty of big western views.

For both thru-hikers and day hikers, what the Arizona Trail offers, what makes it unique, is the immediacy of nature. Conditions that create thorn-covered plants and mule deer that can eat them are harsh and demanding by definition. The extremes along the trail, whether the arctic-like conditions atop the high peaks or the boiling valley floor temperatures of the Sonoran Desert, are equally demanding. What do those conditions do to humans? They bring hikers back to the basics of life: sun, water, air, wind, earth. There is something exhilarating about a connection with nature so fundamental that it is a reminder of what it means to be alive. This is a trail that makes hikers feel those fundamentals, that focuses on them in a way no other trail can.

THE ROUTE

The Arizona Trail is organized into 43 "passages" ranging in length from eight to 31 miles, with the average being around 15 miles long.

Going south to north, the trail starts near the Coronado National Memorial by the Mexican border southeast of Tucson. It winds through the Huachuca Mountains, an important migratory bird corridor. The mountains here have somewhat more reliable water sources than the lower, drier landscape that surrounds them.

Passing through the picturesque small town of Patagonia, the trail then climbs into the Santa Rita Mountains, descends into the historic but now abandoned Kentucky Camp, once the headquarters of the Santa Rita Water and Mining Company, and then enters the Cienega passage, with a few groves of well-watered cottonwoods announcing that this is one of the few places on the trail that has relatively abundant water.

The trail crosses I-10 east of Tucson and enters Saguaro National Park. As it climbs, it leaves behind the saguaros in the park's lower elevations and rises to dry pine forests. Now north of Tucson, the trail climbs into the Rincon and Santa Catalina Mountains, where a small ski area alerts hikers to the expectation of at least some snow and the possibility of frozen springs in winter.

FOLLOWING SPREAD: The Arizona Trail through chain cholla heading toward Battle Axe Butte, White Canyon Wilderness (left); saguaro cacti in bloom above the Gila River near Kelvin, Arizona (top right); Sonoran Desert below the southern cliffs of Copper Butte near Walnut Canyon (bottom right)

The Arizona Trail

Approximately 800 miles from Coronado National Memorial to the Utah border

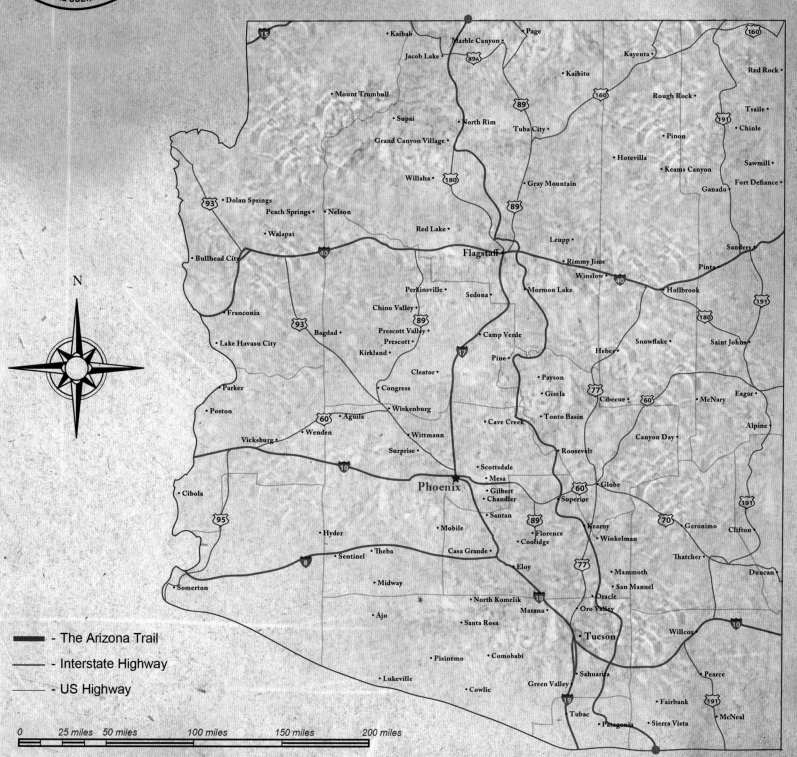

N

- The Arizona Trail
- Interstate Highway
- US Highway

0   25 miles   50 miles   100 miles   150 miles   200 miles

Descending the north side of the Santa Catalinas, the Arizona Trail enters some of the harshest territory in the National Scenic Trails System. To the north of Oracle near Highway 77 is an expanse of Arizona State Trust lands, a rough section of trail with very little water, which on most maps appears as a big empty expanse. Some hikers arrange to stash water caches with the help of local residents or trail volunteers; it's either that or handle multiple 20-plus-mile days between reliable sources. The terrain here is by far the harshest yet encountered, interlaced with jeep roads. Backpackers would probably not choose this section to hike were they not doing the entire trail, but thru-hikers acclimated to the desert find a raw, harsh, windswept wildness here. For some rugged hikers seeking the intensity of natural experience, this section has an allure of its own: it is the kind of country that set Edward Abbey's passion for the desert afire.

The route continues, harsh yet starkly scenic, crossing Highway 60 near Superior, about an hour's drive east of the Phoenix metropolitan area. The craggy Superstition Mountains and the Four Peaks Wilderness Area are said to house a few ghosts. Most definitely, these mountains are inhabited by things that are out to get you: manzanita shrubs, with their red, rubbery, branches that overgrow the trail and catch you as you try to pass; more cholla; and the ubiquitous, persistent catclaw.

North of Roosevelt Lake, the trail follows a dry ridge in the scenic Mazatzal Mountains, then, north of Pine, ascends 3,000 feet up a 200-mile-long escarpment called the Mogollon Rim. Here, the Arizona Trail changes character, reaching the seemingly lush and green Coconino Plateau—a world away from the desert below. What is interesting here is that ecologically speaking Mexico lies at the bottom of the escarpment and the Rocky Mountains lie at the top of it. On the plateau, there is more shade, temperatures are lower, and water can be found at more reasonable intervals. Still, it's worth noting that hikers should not abandon their dryland vigilance of paying attention to water sources: pines are drought tolerant, and water on the ground remains scarce. Forest Service pamphlets contain information like, "Do not be misled by the many lakes pictured on the maps," and, "The water-smoothed stones give one the pleasant feeling of being near a brook even if you have to imagine the babble."

North of the Tonto National Forest and south of Flagstaff, the trail makes a big loop, giving hikers a choice of going east or west around Flagstaff. The landscape here is fairly open, with dramatic jutting rock formations familiar from scenic postcards of the red-rock area around the tourist mecca of Sedona, which lies just to the southwest. This is classic Arizona red-rock country, and accessibility to Sedona makes the Arizona Trail an ideal day trip for visitors.

North of Flagstaff, the trail changes character once again as it heads up to the high country of the San Francisco Peaks, home to Arizona's highest peak. This part of the trail is not passable in the dead of winter; indeed, snow may linger until summer. North of the San Francisco Peaks, a relatively flat stretch along the Coconino Rim takes hikers between Flagstaff and Grand Canyon National Park. Following a combination of hiking trails and jeep roads, the Arizona Trail passes through forests interrupted by open drylands punctuated by rock formations and outcroppings that only hint at what lies ahead.

And then: the Grand Canyon. It really does open up like a cleft in the earth. One minute, you are walking on a flat, forested plain, surrounded by nothing more dramatic than some Ponderosa pines, the next minute, you reach the rim of the canyon and look down into a literal underworld: the two-billion-year-old guts of the earth. The Arizona Trail here follows the well-used mule trails—the South and North Kaibab Trails. For most Arizona Trail hikers, the canyon is a two- or three-day crossing, with a stop at Bright Angel Campground at the bottom, and another possible stop at Cottonwood Campground on the way up to the North Rim.

Much of the Grand Canyon can be hiked in winter, and hiking conditions are comfortable even in January. The exception (for most people) is the North Rim, where all facilities are closed. Trails on the North Rim itself are sometimes used in winter by hardcore snowshoers, but for long-distance hikers, the logistics of getting through here and resupplying in the snowbound months would be impractical.

The trail ends with a relatively easy stretch through little-used arroyo country north to the Utah border through the Kaibab National Forest.

OPPOSITE: Day hikers along the Arizona Trail above Roosevelt Lake, Tonto National Forest (top); Roosevelt Bridge over Roosevelt Lake, Tonto National Forest (bottom)

FOLLOWING SPREAD: Sparse ponderosa forest in Coconino National Forest (top left); the Arizona Trail through an aspen forest along Upper Hart Prairie, San Francisco Peaks, Coconino National Forest (bottom left); San Francisco Peaks framed by piñon pine, Coconino National Forest (right)

OPPOSITE: The Arizona Trail along Kaibab Plateau, Kaibab National Forest

RIGHT: Upper Bright Angel Canyon following the North Kaibab Trail in Grand Canyon National Park (top); lightning storm on Kaibab Plateau, Kaibab National Forest (bottom)

FOLLOWING SPREAD: Vermillion Cliffs near the terminus of the Arizona Trail, Kaibab National Forest

THE ARIZONA TRAIL

The Arizona Trail Association divides the trail into "passages" that can be done as day hikes or weekend backpack trips. The following recommendations showcase the state's variety of ecosystems.

MILLER PEAK, HUACHUCA MOUNTAINS

The Huachuca Mountains, located in the Coronado National Forest near the southern terminus of the Arizona Trail, are an important migratory bird flyway. The range is about 70 miles south of Tucson, and elevations vary a full vertical mile, from 4,000 feet to 9,466 feet atop Miller Peak, the high point of the range (accessible via a side trail from the Arizona Trail). The range is characterized by cliffs, canyons, and biological diversity owing to the range in elevation. Bird-watchers may see several species of hummingbirds, flycatchers, and warblers, as well as trogons and others.

KENTUCKY CAMP, SANTA RITA MOUNTAINS

Accessible from Route 82 southeast of Tucson and north of Patagonia, the historic mining community of Kentucky Camp lies at the northeast side of the Santa Rita Mountains section of the Arizona Trail. From Kentucky Camp, you can head south on the Arizona Trail into sky islands that offer excellent views over southern Arizona and a wide diversity of wildlife, from the expected rattlesnakes and desert hares to the occasional mountain lion.

SAGUARO NATIONAL PARK

For much of southern and central Arizona, the landscape is dominated by saguaro cacti, sentinels of the desert. Along with other giants of the plant kingdom—redwoods and sequoias—saguaros are one of the few species to have a National Park System unit named after them. The trail mostly passes through the higher elevations of the park, where pine trees, not saguaros, are more characteristic. For saguaro sightings, head to the park's lower elevations.

SUPERSTITION AND FOUR PEAKS WILDERNESS AREAS

This backpack trip between Superior and Roosevelt Lakes is one of the toughest stretches of the entire trail, and it is located within an hour's drive of Phoenix. This stark, rugged landscape is best hiked in the cooler months. In late spring and summer, springs are dry, and the heat is frankly dangerous; navigation can also be a challenge. On the north end of the Four Peaks Wilderness, hikers can camp by Roosevelt Lake.

HIGHLINE TRAIL, MOGOLLON RIM

Just south of the Mogollon Rim in the Tonto National Forest, the Arizona Trail follows the Highline Trail. A designated national recreation

trail, the Highline Trail passes through a series of historic homesteads beneath the Mogollon Rim, a 3,000- to 4,000-foot escarpment that cuts across Arizona. To reach the rim, the Arizona Trail then follows the Colonel Devin Trail on a steep ascent through many of the state's environmental zones to finally reach a shady pine-covered plateau. However, water scarcity remains an issue: tourist information about the highlands atop the Mogollon Rim trumpet the fishing and boating opportunities before sheepishly admitting that sometimes the lakes all dry up.

HUMPHREYS PEAK, SAN FRANCISCO PEAKS

North of Flagstaff, this is one of the few places along the Arizona Trail where summer temperatures can be manageable: snow can linger well into June, as can subfreezing temperatures. Humphreys Peak (Arizona's highest at 12,637 feet) is accessible via a side trail. This section is impassible in winter.

SOUTH KAIBAB TRAIL, GRAND CANYON

The obvious, inarguable jewel of the Arizona Trail is the Grand Canyon. From the popular and more accessible South Rim, the Arizona Trail follows the South Kaibab Trail to the Colorado River. This is an overnight hike, not a day hike; day hikers will need to turn back sooner. After a night at Bright Angel Campground, cross-canyon hikers ascend via the North Kaibab Trail; hikers returning to the South Rim can take the less steep Bright Angel Trail through the Indian Garden Campground. This makes for a two-night and three-day trip for most people. Permits are required.

Opposite: Ocotillo in bloom with saguaro cacti near Hope Camp, Saguaro National Park; *Top:* Ruins of Kentucky Camp, Coronado National Forest; *Middle Left:* Rock outcropping, Four Peaks Wilderness, Tonto National Forest; *Middle Right:* Tall cairn on the Arizona Trail, Mogollon Rim, Tonto National Forest; *Bottom:* Hikers along South Kaibab Trail, Grand Canyon National Park

THE PACIFIC NORTHWEST TRAIL

➤ STORY LINES ◄

In the world of Aboriginal Australia, songlines tell the story of paths across the land. Recorded in cultural memory not only as songs, but also as stories, dances, and paintings, songlines tell of routes first taken by the creators of the landscape. The twists and turns of the paths and their stories are reflected in the contours and rhythms of the songs, which, once understood, are as informative as any map. • Across the world, the giant old-growth forests of the Pacific Northwest have little in common with the vast horizons of Australia's outback. In one, dark-green canopies shade a misty, waterlogged world; in the other, red earth bakes under a merciless sun. Could there be anything more different than grizzly bears versus kangaroos, or magical forests of mosses, ferns, and epiphytes versus open, red-hued vistas framed by shimmering blue skies? • What they do have in common is that both landscapes are legendary in scope. In the outback, it is the space itself that is overwhelming—the vistas, skies, horizons. In the Pacific Northwest, it is the forests of sky-blocking monoliths that create a weird and wet understory of life abounding. Legendary landscapes spawn legends, whether tales before time, or tall tales of today—stories of larger-than-life characters in a larger-than-life landscape. Sasquatch comes to mind.

Perhaps it is only right that such stories grow in the fertile Pacific Northwest, a landscape that supports vast understories of symbiotically interwoven life, a tangle of ferns and fungus and fallen trees rotting into moss-covered mats that smell of wet earth and burgeoning life—all topped by giants that throw one's perception of size and scale into a different universe. Like falling down Alice's rabbit hole, the hiker enters a new realm in these temperate rain forests on the flanks of looming volcanoes where trees form sylvan cathedrals, reaching to the heavens every bit as effectively as a Gothic spire.

Yes, the mountains here are impressive—the great, famous volcanoes—but hikers have mountains in abundance on other trails: round green hills in the Appalachians, rocky pinnacles in the land of Colorado's 14ers, dry sky islands in Southern California and Arizona. What *is* exceptional here are the ancient forests that surround the mountains like an apron: thousand-year-old western redcedars, whose trunks can be up to 13 feet in diameter, sometimes more, and towering Douglas firs, the mainstay of the timber industry with their enormous bulk and improbably tiny cones. Not to mention the ecosystems these forests support, and that supports them: the glistening ferns in a thousand shades of green, the salt-tinged coastal rain forests, the thick layers of hummocky organic matter that sustain life but ensnare hiking boots. And perhaps a Sasquatch or two.

In overscale places such as these, as the Australian Aboriginals knew, stories can define the land and guide the visitor through it. So it is fitting that Ron Strickland, the guiding force behind the Pacific Northwest Trail, is a man who is as apt to travel with a tape recorder as a map and notebook. An oral historian whose fascination with stories parallels his fascination with the Pacific Northwest, Strickland has, in this land of deep, unsettled wilderness, found stories of extremes. The trail he has created leads visitors through the secret nooks and crannies of mountain and forest: the haunts of gold miners and

prospectors, renegades and criminals, loggers and woodsmen. In his book, *River Pigs and Cayuses*, Strickland wrote:

> Between 1970 and 1983 I spent as much time as possible exploring and choosing routes for . . . the Pacific Northwest Trail. But soon my fascination with the region grew into a quest to preserve part of the oral traditions I had loved so much as a footloose rambler. Having emigrated from the overdeveloped East, I feared the drastic effects of new roads, summer homes, strip mines, forest rape, water pollution, and other imminent threats. I feared that a time would soon come when so much tradition would be lost that there would be plenty of old people but very few old-timers.

Strickland's journeys to find a route for the trail took him into back-of-beyond communities, where he collected stories for his book. Unlike the songlines of Australia, the stories Strickland collected are not ancient treasures from a time before time: they are living tales, told within living memory. But like songlines, these stories are not only a narrative of lives, but also of the land, and they have a special vocabulary that acts almost as a key to understanding this wild kingdom of giant trees and lonesome spaces that hikers walk through on the Pacific Northwest Trail.

For example, hear the stories of the river pigs. Relatives of neither farmers' pigs nor wild boars, river pigs are young men who do the dangerous work of riding logs downstream and breaking up logjams. Or listen to a Swedish fiddler. He may be completely tone-deaf but it wouldn't matter one whit: his tales are of cutting timber into log lengths. You need a dictionary to understand the language of this land (and Strickland kindly provides one): a misery whip cuts large trees, a cayuse is an Indian pony, and (appropriate for a backpacker) a bindle is a bundle of a wanderer's possessions. There are smoke jumpers and steelheaders and ice harvesters and canoe carvers, moonshiners and river gamblers, snowshoe makers, branding iron makers, refugees, backwoodsmen, a few plain old curmudgeons, and at least a couple of verifiable honest-to-god bad guys.

A walker who knows a little bit about the history of the region—about the intersection of logging camps and mining camps, the isolation of northcountry winters and long distances, the fishing and

PREVIOUS SPREAD: Mokowanis Lake and Glenns Lake near Stoney Indian Pass, Glacier National Park, Montana

OPPOSITE: Stoney Indian Trail section of the PNT, Glacier National Park, Montana

hunting that sustained life—can see the imprint of this history on the land, in the second-growth forests, in the old logging roads, and in the abandoned camps of miners, each one telling of another dream gone bad. The stories Strickland collected interpret the land, and you can almost hear them as you walk. In some cases, you can hear them for real, perhaps in among the larch trees along the North Fork of the Flathead River, where hikers might meet a couple of young homesteaders living without running water until they can afford to put in the plumbing. Or maybe they'll stop to pass some time with an old-timer with a faded voice but unfaded memories of what life was like back when "doing without" somehow made a person richer. The stories one can still hear—of jobs, dangers, challenges, joys—enrich the wanderer with a sense of what it is like to live here, among endless forests of thousand-year-old trees, salmon-stuffed rivers, icy rains, neverending winters, barn raisings, and bee harvesting. In discovering the words of this wilderness and the paths and stories that lead through it, Strickland interpreted the wild lands for his readers. Now, hikers can go out and find, or make, stories of their own.

ONE MAN'S OBSESSION

Like its sibling the Arizona Trail, which also entered the National Scenic Trails System in 2009, the Pacific Northwest Trail is evidence that the quest to build long paths through extraordinary terrain does not belong to the past, but indeed, is, and can be, part of the story of the present.

One of the most interesting trail stories is not one Strickland collected, but one he created: the tale of how a young easterner barely out of college found his life's calling in the wilderness of the Pacific Northwest and created a 1,200-mile-long national scenic trail by means of unstinting devotion over four decades. It is not a unique story. Most of the national scenic trails can trace their genesis to a single (and often single-minded) visionary. But Ron Strickland's tale fits the landscape through which he traveled: out of scale, and a bit bigger than life usually is.

Hard as it may be to hike a long-distance trail, it is even more difficult to create one, and the process becomes more challenging with each passing decade. In his book *Pathfinder*—a memoir that jumbles together seemingly unrelated life events with trail-construction details, philosophy, and, always,

stories—Strickland recalled that the obstacles he encountered along the way were every bit as unpredictable and sometimes mystifying as the obstacles a hiker encounters on an unknown trail. Brimming with enthusiasm over his plans for a 1,200-mile trail in Seattle's beloved backyard wildernesses but unaware of the outdoor politics of the region, he blundered into conflict with organizations from which he may have quite reasonably expected support. His proposal to create a path that mimicked the iconic Pacific Crest Trail drew controversy and—surprisingly—some derision in a community where the PCT was early on regarded as a blight on the land, an invasion of the wilderness, and a place where long-distance hikers were mere showmen and grandstanders.

But Strickland, always a student, was a fast learner: he went "underground," as he called it, striking up unlikely alliances with old-timers who became mentors. He learned not only the lay of the land, but also the labyrinthine networks of organizations and land-management agencies that could help or hinder his effort to create a trail. *Backpacker Magazine* called him a pulpit-pounding evangelist.

In 1980, he ran headlong into a brick wall when the Forest Service and National Park Service published the *Final National Scenic Trail Study Report*. It concluded that, although the proposed Pacific Northwest Trail might cross "some of America's most breathtaking and varied landscapes, it is overwhelmingly evident that development of the trail . . . is neither feasible nor desirable" for reasons ranging from grizzly bear habitat to taxpayer expense.

That conclusion was not "overwhelmingly evident" to Strickland. Undeterred, he kept going. Eventually, he began working with land managers, and with locals who became supporters. Gradually, the trail grew. Strickland published his guidebook in 2001. Hikers started coming. Finally, in 2009, the Pacific Northwest Trail joined the Arizona and New England Trails in becoming the 9th, 10th, and 11th designated national scenic trails.

Strickland's fascination with long-distance trails does not end with the Pacific Northwest Trail. A resident of Boston, he has hiked the also-new New England Trail, and he has been advocating for a connector between the North Country Trail's current western terminus in North Dakota and the eastern terminus of the Pacific Northwest Trail in Glacier National Park—a dream that, if it is ever realized, will

PREVIOUS SPREAD: Kootenai River Valley, Parker Ridge, Kaniksu National Forest, Idaho (left); cairn on Trail 221 along Parker Ridge, Kaniksu National Forest, Idaho (top right); grouse hen near Pyramid Lake, Selkirk Mountains, Kaniksu National Forest, Idaho (middle right); Selkirk Mountains framed by dead spruce, Kaniksu National Forest, Idaho (bottom right)

OPPOSITE: The PNT through old-growth cedar along the Upper Priest River Valley, Kaniksu National Forest, Idaho

result in a trail through the North Country and the Pacific Northwest spanning some 6,000 miles.

And he isn't stopping there. Recently, he has been focusing on an unofficial Atlantic-to-Pacific route that connects Quebec's Atlantic coast with the Olympic Peninsula on the Pacific coast. "It can already be done—following the International Appalachian Trail from Cape Gaspé to the Appalachian Trail, then hiking down through New England and taking the Long Trail up; they still need to connect that with the North Country Trail, but it's being discussed. Then, after you get to North Dakota you still have to make your own route to Glacier National Park, of course—that's where the work needs to be done. But then you get on the Pacific Northwest Trail and follow it to the Pacific."

Only 7,700 miles. Only cut several hundred more miles of trail. As simple as that. But such is the vision that created this trail.

Gargantuan dreams aside, the Pacific Northwest Trail remains at the heart of Strickland's life's work: the grandeur of this landscape, the romance of long-distance trails, and the stories that are tucked away in these mountains and forests. The trail he created acts as a story line from one chapter to the next, revealing and celebrating the secrets hidden, sometimes, in plain sight.

THE ROUTE

Like the other great northern trail—the North Country Trail, far to the east of the Continental Divide—the Pacific Northwest Trail (PNT) follows an east-west orientation. In the Pacific Northwest, that means the trail must transect the dominant north-south orientation of the region's mountain ranges. It would be convenient to imagine that from its start near the Continental Divide to the Pacific Ocean, the journey is all downhill: what a pleasant image for a hiker, to think of oneself as a drop of water, flowing effortlessly from the snowy heights of the Continental Divide down to the salt water of the Pacific Ocean.

But the trail doesn't take that easy way down drainages. Instead, it climbs up and over a series of mountain ranges interspersed with the valleys and forests of Idaho and north-central Washington, where the land supports a variety of traditional rural industries: orchards, forestry, farming, and mining. With the population thin and the mountain ridges high and

isolating, towns only a few miles apart by air may have very different cultures and personalities. Indeed, to walk from one to another on a hiking trail is sometimes the most direct way to get from here to there. This is some of the most remote country in the entire National Scenic Trails System.

From Glacier National Park, the Pacific Northwest Trail heads through western Montana to the Idaho Panhandle, west over the Purcell and Selkirk Mountains, and then into Washington's Okanogan National Forest. It then climbs through the increasingly high and wild Salmo-Priest and Pasayten Wildernesses.

In the Pasayten Wilderness, the Pacific Northwest Trail intersects the Pacific Crest Trail almost at the very north end of the PCT. Descending steeply to Ross Lake, the PNT then follows the shoreline, and, having reached the other side, transects North Cascades National Park and the Mount Baker Wilderness.

Temporarily finished with mountains, the trail descends to cross Puget Sound, where it rejoins civilization in the form of farms, towns, dikes, and a ferry that takes hikers to the Olympic Peninsula and the Hoh Rain Forest. After an oceanside hike, and a crossing of the Quileute Indian Reservation, the trail is finally done at Cape Alava.

En route from Glacier National Park's Continental Divide, where a drop of water might begin its journey, and Cape Alava, where the trail ends at the sea, the Pacific Northwest Trail passes through four states, three national parks, seven national forests, five state parks, and one national historical reserve, in order from east to west: Glacier National Park, Flathead National Forest, Kootenai National Forest, Idaho Panhandle National Forests, Colville National Forest, Okanogan National Forest, North Cascades National Park, Mount Baker-Snoqualmie National Forest, Deception Pass State Park, Bay View State Park, Joseph Whidbey State Park, Fort Ebey State Park, Ebey's Landing National Historical Reserve, Fort Casey State Park, Olympic National Forest, and Olympic National Park.

It is a 1,200-mile cross section of the entire Pacific Northwest region, a land dominated by mountains, water (in the form of snow, ice, thundering rapids, fog, rain, sea spray, and puddles), and, above all, the great old trees. And a few legends, to boot.

FOLLOWING SPREAD: Cathedral Peak and Upper Cathedral Lake, Pasayten Wilderness, Washington (left); Abercrombie Mountain, Colville National Forest, Washington (top right); view south from Abercrombie Mountain, Colville National Forest, Washington (bottom right)

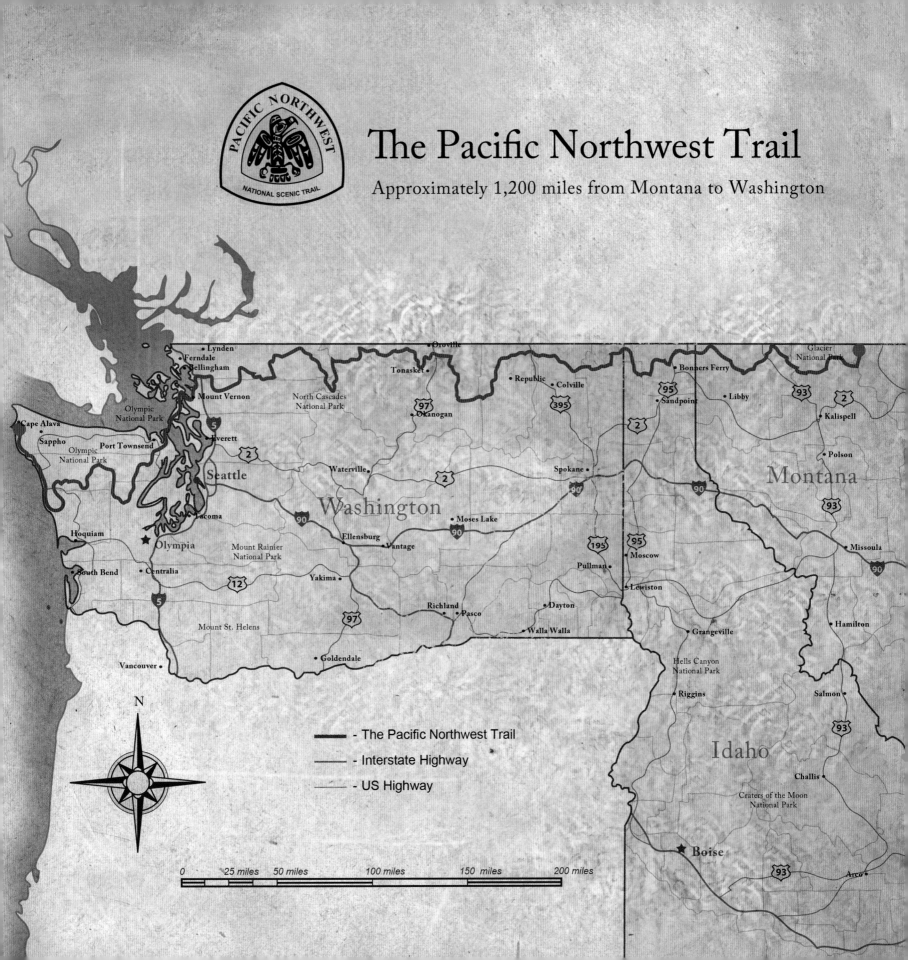

The Pacific Northwest Trail

Approximately 1,200 miles from Montana to Washington

PACIFIC NORTHWEST
NATIONAL SCENIC TRAIL

Washington

Montana

Idaho

Glacier National Park

Olympic National Park

North Cascades National Park

Mount Rainier National Park

Mount St. Helens

Hells Canyon National Park

Craters of the Moon National Park

Lynden · Ferndale · Bellingham · Mount Vernon · Everett · Seattle · Tacoma · Olympia · Centralia · South Bend · Hoquiam · Cape Alava · Sappho · Port Townsend · Vancouver

Oroville · Tonasket · Republic · Colville · Okanogan · Waterville · Spokane · Moses Lake · Ellensburg · Vantage · Yakima · Richland · Pasco · Dayton · Walla Walla · Goldendale

Bonners Ferry · Sandpoint · Libby · Kalispell · Polson · Missoula · Moscow · Pullman · Lewiston · Grangeville · Riggins · Salmon · Hamilton · Challis · Boise · Arco

95 · 93 · 2 · 97 · 395 · 90 · 195 · 12 · 5

N

- The Pacific Northwest Trail
- Interstate Highway
- US Highway

0   25 miles   50 miles   100 miles   150 miles   200 miles

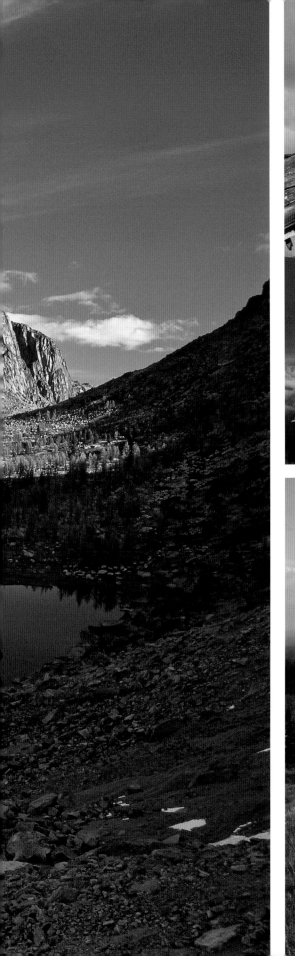

LEFT: Hiker heading south along the PCT above Devils Stairway on the PNT, Pasayten Wilderness, Washington (top); the PNT heading down Devils Dome toward Ross Lake, North Cascade Mountains, Pasayten Wilderness, Washington (bottom)

OPPOSITE: Nooksack Cirque from Hannegan Peak, North Cascades National Park, Washington

FOLLOWING SPREAD: Boulders in Gray Wolf River, Buckhorn Wilderness, Washington (left); the PNT near Gray Wolf River, Buckhorn Wilderness, Washington (right)

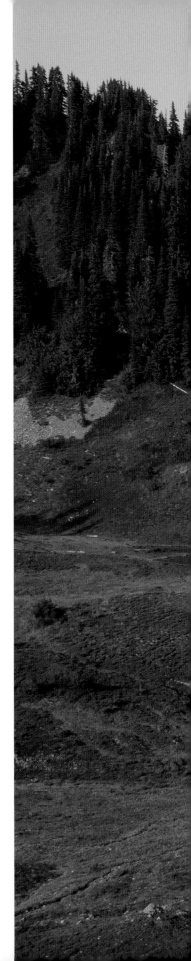

THE PACIFIC NORTHWEST TRAIL

For the Pacific Northwest Trail highlights, Ron Strickland suggested his favorites, choosing trails that reflect the variety along the PNT, many of which are accessible to day hikers and backpackers on shorter journeys. Most of these hikes are described in Strickland's 2001 book, *Pacific Northwest Trail Guide*, and in Tim Youngbluth's 2013 book, *Pacific Northwest Trail Digest*.

GLACIER NATIONAL PARK, GOAT HAUNT RANGER STATION (Montana)

This hike begins on the shores of Waterton Lake near the international border between the United States and Canada under the shadow of the Continental Divide. From the Canadian side of Waterton Lake, take the boat to Goat Haunt and then stride out: to the south, the Continental Divide Trail will lead to Mexico, to the west, the PNT will lead to the Pacific Ocean. Or, more reasonably, take an out-and-back day hike to Brown Pass.

KOOTENAI NATIONAL FOREST, WEBB MOUNTAIN (Montana)

A 3,600-foot climb to the Webb Mountain Lookout, 6.3 miles from the trailhead, makes a good day hike for those strong enough to handle the mileage and elevation gain.

COLVILLE NATIONAL FOREST, CENTRAL KETTLE RANGE (Washington)

Boulder Creek Road and State Route 20 both cross the north-south-running Kettle Range. In between them is a 28.6-mile stretch, perfect for a weekend trip. The relatively gentle mountains here are remote and little visited. If you look closely in spring, you may see orchids.

OKANOGAN NATIONAL FOREST, MOUNT BONAPARTE (Washington)

This moderate 16.4-mile hike takes hikers to the tallest mountain in northeastern Washington, and offers excellent views of the Okanogan National Forest. Start at Bonaparte Lake Campground, and take the side trail to the summit of Mount Bonaparte via Lookout Trail No. 306. The 16-mile section between roads ends at Swanson Mill County Road No. 4662.

OKANOGAN NATIONAL FOREST, WHISTLER CANYON (Washington)

This easy 14.8-mile section between Whistler Canyon Road No. 100 and the town of Oroville is a microcosm of the contrasts on the Pacific Northwest Trail. The dry Okanogan slopes contrast with the green farmlands, fields, and orchards in the agricultural lands below; settled communities exist on the edge of backcountry.

OKANOGAN NATIONAL FOREST, EASTERN PASAYTEN WILDERNESS (Washington)

The PNT's 79.6-mile route through the eastern Pasayten Wilderness is one of the top long backpack trips of the entire National Scenic Trails System. It features unbroken stretches of wilderness and mountain views. Bauerman Ridge and Bunker Hill are highlights.

ROSS LAKE NATIONAL RECREATION AREA (Washington)

The Ross Lake National Recreation Area is easily accessible by road. To the east lies the Okanogan National Forest, to the west the backcountry of North Cascades National Park. At Ross Lake, day hikers can strike out on the PNT from Big Beaver Campground. Backpackers can head from Ross Dam to Ruth Creek. Long-distance hikers can head west to the Pacific Ocean or east to the

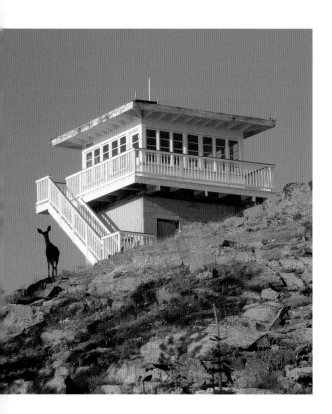

Continental Divide. Or they can climb up to the Pacific Crest Trail above Ross Lake and turn south to Mexico.

CHUCKANUT DRIVE, BLANCHARD HILL (Washington)

This four-mile round-trip through land managed by the Washington State Department of Natural Resources has panoramic views of the San Juan Islands, Samish Bay, Olympic Mountains, Skagit Flats, and Mount Rainier. It's not only a synopsis of the Pacific Northwest, but also an important historic marker for the trail: in 1982, this was the first piece of trail to be newly constructed specifically for inclusion in what was then a pie-in-the-sky Pacific Northwest Trail. Strickland recommends that day hikers park on Chuckanut Drive just south of the guardrail near the Oyster Bar restaurant—and dine at one of the local Chuckanut Drive restaurants after the hike.

OLYMPIC NATIONAL PARK (Washington)

The 22.3-mile walk between La Push and Cape Alava is mostly a wilderness beach walk to a remote inaccessible area, known as a former whale-hunting center. Among the sounds and spray of pounding surf, look for whales, otters, seals, and sea lions. Landward, you might see bears; skyward, you might spot bald eagles and ospreys. If you've been walking east to west, finally, you have nowhere else to go. If you're just starting, the wonders of the Pacific Northwest Trail lie just ahead. And for the short-term hiker, this stretch of wild beach between La Push and Cape Alava might just get you thinking of far horizons.

Opposite: Fire lookout atop Webb Mountain along the PNT, Kootenai National Forest; *Top:* Sea lion near Scotts Bluff, Olympic National Park; *Bottom:* Section of the PNT along Chuckanut Mountain

THE
NEW ENGLAND
TRAIL

Among the giants of the national scenic trails, the New England Trail stands out as a bit of an anomaly. At 215 miles, it is the shortest of the long-distance trails. It is the only national scenic trail with neither a national park nor a national forest along its route. And, in terms of dramatic scenery, the contained and civilized landscapes of the Northeast are dwarfed by the wild and mighty monoliths of the western trails. (Think Emily Dickinson versus John Muir.) • Yet there is a quiet beauty to this corner of the world: the Connecticut River Valley of south-central New England may be a mere two or three hours from New York City, but in winter, Long Island Sound harbors seals and migrating birds. The world-famous New England foliage along the Connecticut River is set off against bucolic farmlands with neat red barns and rolls of hay. Some of the towns are among the oldest settlements in America; these are places that spawned the ideas that helped shape governments and philosophies—including the ideas that helped form the outdoor recreation movement as it is known today. And the National Scenic Trails System.

The New England Trail (NET) challenges and expands the idea of what a national scenic trail is, and what it is for. For many hikers, one of the first questions is length: all of the other national scenic trails are longer. Most are 800 miles or more, with the North Country Trail topping the list with its almost unimaginable 4,600 miles. But contrary to popular assumption, length is not the primary determining factor in deciding whether or not a trail can be considered for national scenic trail status. Instead, to make the cut, trails must meet certain other standards in terms of recreational values, trail quality, and community support.

It's interesting to note that there are several dozen hiking trails between 200 and 400 miles in length in the National Trails System designated as national recreation trails. National recreation trails recognize and protect paths that have superlative regional, scenic, or recreational values. And while managers of some of those other trails have considered seeking national scenic trail status, the fact is that only one of these "short-long trails"—the New England Trail—has, at least so far, actually been designated a national scenic trail.

To understand why this makes sense, one needs to consider what is special about this path through some of the oldest settlements in America. The title of a book by one of New England's native sons, Henry David Thoreau's *Faith in a Seed*, offers some clues. As it turns out, some of the philosophical seeds that were planted in New England's rocky, frostbitten soil grew into ideas that created what is now the National Trails System, a network encompassing more than 60,000 miles of trails.

Located smack in the middle of southern New England and running through or past 41 communities on its 215-mile route—mathematically, that's one community for every five miles of trail—the New England Trail is never more than a three-hour drive from the entire population of Connecticut, Massachusetts, Rhode Island, and most of the New York metropolitan area. The NET thus meets one of the stated goals of the National Trails System Act: to bring trails to where the people are. This accessibility gives the trail a strong population base from which to recruit volunteers, who are so important to the maintenance of any long-distance trail.

Yet even though the trail traverses a densely populated area (by long-distance trail standards), its terrain is bucolic and gently pretty, a landscape that nurtures rather than challenges. Olde New England still lives, even this close to the cities: ridges overlook broad river valleys, small towns give way to big farms, and large tracts of forest lands contain all manner of small wonders—waterfalls and streams, shady glades, and sunlit summits. While the trail stays calmly within its ecozone—no manic swings from desert to tundra are to be found here—there is variety on a small scale, both historic and natural, including the saltwater marshlands of Long Island Sound, the historic markers dating to colonial times, the small differences in the composition of forests, and changing ecosystems due to differences in elevation and sunlight, even if the variations don't often exceed 1,000 feet.

And then there are the seasons, all four of them equally represented: the folded and undulating blankets of snow; the bright hopeful greens of spring; the lazy hazes of summer; and the brilliant hues of New England autumn punctuated by sharp blue skies and white-steepled churches. Like a tiny seed, the New England Trail has everything it needs—just in miniature.

And this smaller scale also offers another benefit to the hiking community. The National Scenic Trails System contains only 11 national scenic trails. It is an elite, rigorously selected group. Given the quality of these trails, backpacking any one of them is a bucket-list type of trip. But relatively few people can spend the many months it takes first to plan a thru-hike of a thousand miles or more—and then to complete the hike itself. The New England Trail is much more manageable. The presence of towns at frequent intervals along the way makes resupply easy, and offers an experience that swings between backcountry and small-town America. And, while a hike of 215 miles is nothing to sneeze at—to the contrary, completing a trail of that length is a massive achievement, far more than the vast majority of people will ever walk in one stretch—it doesn't require quitting your job and moving out of your house. Too, hiking a trail like this can be an introductory hike for those planning to move on to longer trails sometime in the future. In any case, the satisfaction of completing an entire

national scenic trail can lead to future hiking endeavors, involvement in the trail community as a donor or volunteer, and a commitment to preserving trails and the lands through which they pass.

GROWING THE TRAIL

The New England Trail has a somewhat different history than almost all the other national scenic trails. Most of the rest of the trails had their genesis in the dreams of one or two visionaries and activists, followed by decades of sorting out the routing and resolving the many land-management issues that surround putting an actual trail on the ground. In contrast, much of what is now the New England Trail has existed as marked hiking footway for more than 50 years, and some segments date back hundreds of years to Native American travel routes. Until its designation in 2009, however, it was a little-known collection of regional trails better known by the traditional names of its major components: the Mattabesett, Metacomet, and Monadnock Trails.

The desire to protect those existing trails was the impetus that created the New England Trail. In a region of ever-increasing development and density, designation as a national scenic trail was seen as a preservation strategy. Association with the National Park Service, which was designated the lead federal agency for this trail, gave the NET more resources, including the funds to hire a trail planner to coordinate and collaborate with agencies and organizations such as the Appalachian Mountain Club and the Connecticut Forest and Park Association, and to work with landowners along the route.

Because most of its route was already on the ground, the NET did not require the kind of massive easement negotiation that has challenged proponents of other trails, not to mention the Pulaski-in-hand kind of pioneering work taken on by Myron Avery on the Appalachian Trail or Ron Strickland on the Pacific Northwest Trail. However, some relocations to preexisting routes were made, and new trail was created on the southern end to connect the Mattabesett Trail to Long Island Sound. On the northern end, the trail officially stops at the New Hampshire border, although hikers interested in continuing even farther into northern New England can then hop on the Monadnock Trail to Mount Monadnock in southern New Hampshire. From there, yet more connections can be made, first to the 48-mile Monadnock-Sunapee Greenway, followed by the 75-mile Sunapee Ragged Kearsage Greenway.

The era for developing and creating new long-distance trails and new routes is far from over. The act that created the New England Trail left the northern terminus undetermined: it is possible that sometime in the future the trail may continue on.

UNDER THE MAGNIFYING GLASS

You cannot examine a gigantic mountain range with a magnifying glass: that is not what mountain ranges, or magnifying glasses, are for. But, if you apply the metaphorical magnifying glass to the comparatively miniature New England Trail and its small mountains, you may perhaps see much more than you anticipated. Like the tiny seed in which Thoreau put so much faith, the New England Trail has much more than at first meets the eye: it is not only an entire microcosm of what a national scenic trail is, but also the origin of the American outdoors, wilderness, and long-distance hiking movements.

And, just like a brave little seedling venturing forth despite the possibility of a late-spring snowstorm, the New England Trail seems at first a bit misplaced. One expects that ideas essential to the creation of the contemporary wilderness and environmental movements were spawned in a wild and larger-than-life location—California's High Sierra, perhaps. In fact, New England was not only equally important to the national trails movement; it was on the scene first. But how was that idea born, here in the densely populated Northeast, in this landscape shaded by afternoon shadows of the traprock ridges that frame the New England Trail?

To answer, you must travel back in time to the mid-19th century. The Industrial Revolution was in full swing, creating railroads, building factories, developing new industries, enlarging cities, shoving newly arrived workers into slums, and escorting newly minted millionaires into mansions. Among all of this sprouted a seed as out of place as a cactus in a cornfield. Southern New England was the center of a new philosophical movement, transcendentalism, led by people like Ralph Waldo Emerson and Henry David Thoreau, who combined mysticism and romanticism and sought revelation by interacting with divine Nature with a capital *N*. Thoreau built his cabin at Walden Pond; his writing told the world that walking in nature was an almost sacred route

to enlightenment. He came close to the soul of wildness atop Katahdin in Maine and returned to the lowlands shaken and changed.

At the same time, New England was home to another relatively recent development: the idea of tourism for pleasure. Travel, remember, takes its root from "travail." A special combination of factors was required to move it from the category of "pain" to the category of "pleasure" in the human experience. First, there had to be new technology, which brought faster modes of transportation. At the same time, the shift had to occur in a place where distances were small enough for travel at a 19th-century pace and varied enough that a day's journey could take one to something new and different, from cities to oceans or mountains. And, there had to be an impetus—a reason to travel—perhaps the need to escape from increasing urbanization, from stress, from noise, from the ceaseless barrage of motion at the new, unhuman pace of machines and steam engines. These factors came together in New England, which once again became, in the recreation movement as in so many others, a crucible.

Trails were then only a new idea: the Crawford Path up New Hampshire's Mount Washington was built in 1819 as a feature for inn guests who wanted to experience the mountain (it may be the oldest recreational hiking trail still in use today). The Long Trail, conceived just after the turn of the century, became the nation's first long-distance hiking path when the Green Mountain Club was formed in 1910. Along what is today the New England Trail, so-called mountain houses built in the 1800s gave visitors the chance to climb relatively modest peaks like Mount Tom or Mount Holyoke and return to sleep and eat in the comforts of a rustic lodge.

The two organizations that have lead roles in maintaining today's New England Trail—the Appalachian Mountain Club and the Connecticut Forest and Park Association—were founded in the late 1800s, as was the Trustees of Reservations, which was formed to preserve scenic and historic landscapes. The outdoor recreation movement spread to cities, both in New England and elsewhere, with the work of Frederick Law Olmsted—who, in his Brookline, Massachusetts, office, was busy planning not only Boston's "Emerald Necklace," but also parks from Montreal to Yosemite, New York to Chicago, along with parkways that, in one of the first examples of

OPPOSITE: Mountain laurel in Penwood State Park along the Metacomet Trail section of the NET, Connecticut

FOLLOWING SPREAD: The Metacomet Trail section of the NET along Rattlesnake Mountain, Connecticut (left); rock sculptures in Penwood State Park along the Metacomet Trail section of the NET, Connecticut (right)

multiple-use planned development, included river protection, scenic carriage rides, walking, and conservation as part of their missions.

From all of this, there is an obvious and direct line to another New England native son, Benton MacKaye, whose proposal for an Appalachian Trail and the solution it offered to the "problem of living" led to the long-distance hiking movement. It seems fitting that MacKaye's home in Shirley, Massachusetts, is a mere 50 miles from today's New England Trail. And it seems no accident that in the shadow of the modest ridges that line the Connecticut River exists the genesis of the long-distance trail movement. The earliest long-distance hiking trails were conceived and first planned and laid out in this region; the idea spread nationwide, and then returned to New England as the nation's youngest national scenic trail, along which some of the oldest recreational hiking trails can be found.

THE ROUTE

The New England Trail offers both an exploration of history and of nature. For its entire length, the trail runs on a twisting course that is roughly parallel to the Connecticut River, New England's largest and longest. It passes through 41 communities, many of which have been settled since the 17th century. The trail stays on the river's western side through all of Connecticut and almost halfway through Massachusetts. Between Holyoke and Northampton, it crosses to the eastern side for the remainder of Massachusetts, up to its terminus at the New Hampshire border.

The trail starts about 20 miles west of the mouth of the Connecticut River in Chittenden Park just south of Guilford, Connecticut, first settled in 1639. Heading north from Long Island Sound, the trail follows a newly constructed 16-mile spur called the Menunkatuck, built to connect the preexisiting Mattabesett Trail to Long Island Sound.

From Guilford, the New England Trail is contiguous with the Mattabesett Trail. The Mattabesett splits in southern Connecticut, where a spur deviates northeast to a terminus on the Connecticut River just downstream from Middletown. The main trail continues northwest, and, near Meriden, joins the Metacomet Trail. The Metacomet, per its name (after a Native American chief who famously led and then died in an uprising against British colonists in New England), spends most of its time on the Metacomet

Ridge, a traprock ridge several hundred feet above the valley that forms the spine of southern New England.

This part of New England is notable for its microclimates. Driving a mere few miles from one town to another, or hiking a few hundred feet up or down a ridge, a visitor can observe an entirely different ecosystem: mountain laurel highlands, white pine forests, shaded riverine habitats, open valley fields with vernal pools, and swamp floodplains. On the Metacomet Ridge, the rocky slopes support a series of isolated microclimates caused by differences in soil drainage and soil type. Habitats range from sun-loving oak savannas to cool damp groves shaded by Eastern hemlocks. Above, raptors and other migrating birds find air currents to ride over the dramatically layered sedimentary rock cliffs that look like a giant layer cake that was baked at the wrong angle. The natural history here is long and rich: some of those layers contain dinosaur tracks.

In Massachusetts, the trail becomes the Metacomet-Monadnock Trail, which will continue to follow the Metacomet Ridge overlooking Pioneer Valley (the local name for the Connecticut River Valley). Within easy access to Hartford, Connecticut, and Springfield, Massachusetts (and almost underneath the flight path of airplanes coming into Bradley International Airport, making the trail accessible to visitors from out of the region), the trail is both rugged and scenic, with rocky scrambles and outlooks offering views east to the Connecticut River Valley and west to the Berkshires.

Leaving the ridge in central Massachusetts, the trail approaches the Connecticut River, and now its route seems intent on passing through as many state parks, forests, and reservations as possible. The series of public lands stacked almost one after the other begins with Mount Tom State Reservation on the river's western side, followed by a climb up to the jutting ridgeline of Skinner State Park on the eastern side, immediately followed by Mount Holyoke Range State Park. From here, the trail enters a patchwork of state and private land, passing through Shutesbury State Forest, Lake Wyola State Park, Wendell State Forest, Erving State Forest, Northfield State Forest, and Mount Grace State Forest. The New England Trail ends in the middle of nowhere, just north of the Royalston State Forest at the New Hampshire border. Marked hiking trail, however, continues northeast to Monadnock . . . and beyond.

The New England Trail

Approximately 215 miles from
Long Island Sound to the
New Hampshire border

─── - The New England Trail

─── - Interstate Highway

─── - US Highway

N

0   5 miles 10 miles   20 miles   40 miles

Manchester Center •

Grafton •

• Bellows Falls

• Jamaica

• Walpole

Gilsum •

• Stoddard

Vermont

New Hampshire

• Sunderland

Putney •

• Keene

• Shaftsbury

Marlborough •

West Dover •

• Wilmington

• Brattleboro

• Troy

7 Bennington

West Brattleboro •

202

Pownal •   Stamford •   • Readsboro

• Hinsdale

• Winchester

• North Adams

Winchendon •

7

• Adams

Baldwinville •

Greenfield •

Orange •

Millers Falls •

Gardner •

202

• South Deerfield

Massachusetts

Barre •

Hatfield •   • Amherst

Rutland •

Lenox •

91

Northampton •

90

Easthampton •

Ware •

20

• Warren

• Housatonic

• Holyoke

90

7

• Three Rivers

• Great Barrington

90

West Springfield •   **Springfield**

• Longmeadow

84

Canaan •

Quinebaug •

North Granby •   • Hazardville

202   202

44

Granby •   Crystal Lake •   South Woodstock •

• Winsted   91   Windsor Locks •

Tariffville •

7

Ellington •   84   44

91   5

Weatogue •   • Storrs

Collinsville •   • Coventry   6

Torrington •   **Hartford** ★

84

• Kent   Bantam •   • Litchfield   • Wethersfield   • Willimantic

202   Terryville •   South Windham •

New Preston •   • Bristol   • New Britain   • Terramuggus

6   • Middletown   Jewett City •

• Oakville   • Southington   • Colchester

Meriden •

84   Cheshire •   5   91   Moodus •   • Norwich

7   • Naugatuck   395

• Durham

Connecticut   • Uncasville

• Danbury   • Seymour   North Haven •   1

Shelton •   • Ansonia   1

Derby •   **New Haven** •

• Branchville   Guilford •

7   • Trumbull

• Aspetuck

THE NEW ENGLAND TRAIL

As is appropriate for a trail steeped in history, highlights of the New England Trail include both natural attractions of views and ridges, and man-made additions to the landscape, including one of the oldest mountain houses in the region.

CHITTENDEN PARK AT LONG ISLAND SOUND (Connecticut)
The start of the trail at this state park on Long Island Sound is a favorite place for walkers, beach lovers, bird-watchers, fishermen, and now hikers. A new boardwalk makes the beach accessible to handicapped visitors, and offers views of Faulkner Island and Chaffinch Island Park.

HUBBARD PARK OF THE HANGING HILLS OF MERIDEN (Connecticut)
This park on the Metacomet Trail in central Connecticut is crowned by the Castle Craig observation tower. At 976 feet, the tower looks over the Quinnipiac River Valley and all the way back to Long Island Sound. Designed with the help of landscape architect Frederick Law Olmsted, the park contains a large flower garden, picnic areas, and a venue for outdoor concerts—as well as a rumored canine spirit known as the Black Dog of the Hanging Hills.

HEUBLEIN TOWER (Connecticut)
This 165-foot-tall tower in Talcott Mountain State Park looks out over the Hartford skyline and the Farmington River Valley. The expansive views are especially beautiful in the fall.

MOUNT TOM (Massachusetts)
At 1,202 feet, this northern Massachusetts traprock mountain peak looks much bigger than it actually is as it rises above the Connecticut River Valley near Holyoke, Massachusetts. It's the highest peak on the Metacomet Ridge, and has excellent views, a network of hiking trails, and prime spots for watching migrating raptors.

HOLYOKE RANGE (Massachusetts)
Like nearby Mount Tom, the Holyoke Range (also called the Mount Holyoke Range), is part of the traprock Metacomet Ridge over the Connecticut River. This popular hiking area is known for its high rocky ledges that look out over the surrounding valleys and its open views. The Mount Holyoke Summit House, built in 1821, was one of the first mountain houses in the region, and has recently been renovated and is now open to visitors.

MOUNT MONADNOCK (New Hampshire)
This New Hampshire mountain is not on the New England Trail, but hikers can easily reach it by continuing on the Metacomet-Monadnock Trail north of the New Hampshire border. The peak is one of the most famous hiking destinations in southern New Hampshire; it seems a shame to leave it out of this collection simply because of a state border.

Left: Forest along Mount Holyoke Range on the Monadnock Trail section of the NET; *Opposite:* Dramatic traprock outcropping on Mount Tom along the Monadnock Trail section of the NET

TRAILS TO NEW HORIZONS

So where should you walk from here?   •   The National Trails System is a system built on dreams. And, like dreams, it is open ended. As time passes and new visionaries come up with new ideas for where new trails might wander, yet more routes will be added to the system. And there are plenty of trails waiting in the wings.   •   Rich as the National Trails System is, it's only part of the great network of long trails that offer recreational opportunities in every ecosystem, environment, and geological zone of the United States. And while grand dreams, grand trails, and grand achievements always receive the most media hype, it's worth noting that the vast majority of people using the National Scenic Trails System are out for much shorter journeys—a week or two, a weekend, or, most common of all, a simple day hike. Congress did not create national scenic trails to give a few thousand people a chance to become celebrities in the tiny fishbowl world of long-distance hiking. It created the

system to serve as a resource for both Americans and international visitors to experience America, whether in their backyards or across the country.

This chapter explores a sampling of other long trails that offer superior hiking experiences, some of which may one day become national scenic trails. Included are a few well-known trails that are in large part already contiguous with some of the national scenic trails, but that have their own identities and histories. As discrete units with their own merits, these trails, with their comparatively manageable lengths, offer more people the opportunity to complete a long-distance trail in its entirety. This collection also includes other notable long trails that showcase a variety of environments, locations, and types of hiking. Some are complete with blazes, clear footways, maps, and guidebooks. Others are still in development, but they have communities of volunteers, advocates, and users, and most of their routes are currently hikeable.

Some of these trails are already in the National Trails System as designated national recreation trails. This category of trails was added to the system in 1978 to recognize trails that were of exemplary local or regional value. It includes not only hiking trails, but also bike paths, equestrian trails, and water trails. The American Hiking Society maintains a database of more than 1,225 national recreation trails.

Finally, this chapter takes a look at some of the megatrails—the trails that grab newspaper headlines and fuel dreams of spending months or a year in backcountry. In many cases, these superlong routes are combinations or networks of already existing trails. For all practical purposes, these are trails of dreams: only a handful of über-enthusiasts will attempt, let alone finish, something like an ocean-to-ocean hike. Still, a hiker can dream.

And dreaming is, in the end, at the heart of America's great long trails: conceiving of them, putting in the decades of work that it takes to build them, protecting them and the environment surrounding them—and hiking them.

This chapter is not meant to be a complete list of American hiking trails, but rather a taste of what awaits day hikers, backpackers, and thru-hikers throughout the country.

PREVIOUS SPREAD: The Colorado Trail heading toward Kennebec Pass, Cumberland Basin

OPPOSITE: Cathedral Peak reflected in Upper Cathedral Lake, John Muir Trail, Yosemite National Park, California

NOTABLE LONG TRAILS

The decision of which trails to feature here was based on several factors: where each trail is located, its scenic and recreational resources, and how much of the trail currently exists on the ground, ready to be hiked. The result is a mix that represents the variety of experiences the National Scenic Trails System seeks to protect: not only mountains and jungles, deserts and forests, but also trails close to cities and trails in the deep backcountry.

Most of the following trails are at least 150 miles long, although some slightly shorter trails received so many accolades from so many long-distance hikers that they snuck under the wire. (And a few much shorter trails received so many votes and are so unique that they are included here in a special wild card category.) Note that there are some discrepancies regarding the trail lengths: the American Hiking Society's database, as well as information from the trail organizations responsible for maintaining and managing each trail, were used as sources for these lengths.

ALLEGHENY TRAIL
(Pennsylvania, West Virginia, and Virginia)

The Allegheny Trail is an almost-completed 330-mile hiking trail that is slated to become part of a new Great Eastern Trail, a megatrail that will run vaguely parallel to and to the west of the Appalachian Trail from New York to Alabama. The route of the Allegheny Trail follows the Allegheny Mountains, which are a west-central subrange of the Appalachian Mountains. It extends from the Mason-Dixon Line at the Pennsylvania-West Virginia border south to the Appalachian Trail on Peters Mountain on the border of Virginia and West Virginia. On its journey through the Allegheny Highlands, it traverses the Monongahela National Forest in West Virginia and the George Washington and Jefferson National Forests in Virginia.

BAY AREA RIDGE TRAIL (California)

The Bay Area Ridge Trail is a planned 550-plus-mile trail that follows the hills and mountain ridges surrounding the San Francisco Bay area. Currently, more than 330 miles are complete. Designed as a multiuse nonmotorized path for hikers, runners, mountain bicyclists, and equestrians, the trail will connect more than 75 parks and open spaces.

BAY CIRCUIT TRAIL (Massachusetts)

The Bay Circuit Trail runs a ring around the outer Boston suburbs for 200 miles, most of which are completed. First proposed in 1928, the trail was conceived as a suburban companion to the "Emerald Necklace"—Boston's famed urban park network designed by Frederick Law Olmsted. The Bay Circuit Trail passes through 50 towns and cities, as well as conservation lands, nature sanctuaries, national historic parks, state parks, and other green spaces. From beaches to cranberry bogs, salt marshes to woodlands, river corridors, swamps, and lakes to historic sites and museums, and past glacial features such as kettles, drumlins, and eskers, the loop showcases an immense variety of habitats and ecosystems within an easy drive or public transportation ride of the Boston metropolitan area.

BENTON MACKAYE TRAIL
(Georgia, Tennessee, and North Carolina)

Honoring Appalachian Trail founder Benton MacKaye, this eponymous trail is a nearly 300-mile footpath in the southern Appalachian Mountains from Springer Mountain (the southern terminus of the AT) to Great Smoky Mountains National Park. It passes through eight designated wildernesses or wilderness study areas in Georgia, Tennessee, and North Carolina. More remote and less used than the Appalachian Trail, the Benton MacKaye Trail provides an excellent alternative for hikers seeking a more solitary experience in the southern Appalachians.

BUCKEYE TRAIL (Ohio)

The Buckeye Trail is a gigantic 1,444-mile loop around Ohio. This is a long-distance trail, but it is perhaps best suited for short-distance use: most hikers with time to hike 1,400 miles are going to choose a more secluded backcountry experience. But this trail is ideal for day hikers and short-term backpackers. The Buckeye Trail's 26 sections, averaging a manageable 55 miles each, offer access to recreational walking, biking, and hiking paths all over the state. And the range of experiences is broader than one might expect, encompassing historic and prehistoric sites; urban, rural, and suburban hiking trails ranging from towpaths to bike paths to foot-trails to country roads to sidewalks; a sampling of the state's ecosystems; and a few truly travel-worthy outdoor destinations such as Hocking Hills State Park in the southeast of the state. The North Country Trail is contiguous with the Buckeye Trail for much of

OPPOSITE: A blue blaze along the Buckeye Trail near Fort Loromie, Ohio

its circular route through Ohio, following it down the eastern side of the state, looping along the bottom, and then going back up the western side.

CENTENNIAL TRAIL (South Dakota)

This 111-mile trail through the Black Hills and prairies of South Dakota covers some of the terrain first explored by Custer's Black Hills Expedition of 1874. The northern terminus is located atop 4,422-foot Bear Butte, a sacred Native American spot. It comes within one mile of Mount Rushmore, and then heads to its southern terminus at Wind Cave National Park.

COHOS TRAIL (New Hampshire)

The Cohos Trail is a 162-mile trail in northern New Hampshire that stretches across the state's most remote and unpopulated terrain. Some advocates for the New England Trail hope that at some point in the future the NET might extend through New Hampshire all the way to Canada, perhaps by linking with the Cohos Trail and other already-in-place New Hampshire trails.

COLORADO TRAIL (Colorado)

The Colorado Trail runs 500 miles from Denver to Durango through six wilderness areas and eight spectacular mountain ranges. The middle portion of the Colorado Trail is mostly contiguous with the Continental Divide Trail, although in some sections the Continental Divide Trail Society, which publishes a series of CDT guidebooks, recommends a different route.

The Colorado Trail was formed as a grassroots statewide effort, conceived by Bill Lucas and Merrill Hastings of *Colorado Magazine*, and led in large part by trail advocate Gudy Gaskill. The mission of the trail was a populist one: to create a trail through high scenic country accessible to a wide variety of outdoor enthusiasts, not just superfit long-distance hikers. The trail thus tries to avoid as much as possible some of the serious dangers of above-tree-line travel, such as the daily summer thunderstorms that can trap hikers on high exposed ridges with nowhere to turn for shelter. Even so, its high point—13,271 feet, just below the 13,334-foot Coney Summit—is nothing to take lightly, and the average elevation of the trail is more than 10,000 feet, with a total elevation gain of 89,354 feet over the course of its 500 miles.

The trail's routing was also developed with some amount of accessibility in mind: the Colorado

OPPOSITE: The Colorado Trail through a meadow near Horseshoe Gulch

FOLLOWING SPREAD: The Colorado Trail through a lodgepole pine forest, Lost Creek Wilderness (top left); bighorn sheep, Waterton Canyon Trail section of the Colorado Trail near Denver (middle left); the Colorado Trail heading toward Rolling Mountain, San Juan National Forest (bottom left); moose in a pond along Elk Creek, Weminuche Wilderness, Colorado (right)

Trail Foundation organizes supported group hikes with vans that meet hikers at the end of the day with supplies and camping equipment. The trail is also sometimes a shared-use path for hikers, stock users, and cyclists; in wilderness sections, where bicycles are not permitted, the Colorado Trail Foundation provides maps and alternate routes for cyclists.

CUMBERLAND TRAIL (Tennessee)

Beginning at the Cumberland Gap National Historical Park, the single-track Cumberland Trail follows a line of ridges and gorges along the eastern escarpment of the Cumberland Plateau in Tennessee. The route commemorates one of the most important passes through the mountains that allowed early explorers and settlers to move west. It ends just outside Chattanooga, Tennessee. More than 300 miles of trail are planned; about 200 miles have been completed thus far. The route has been chosen to maximize highlights such as remote gorges, scenic waterfalls, and swimming holes, along with overlooks and other water sources. The trail will eventually become part of the Great Eastern Trail.

FINGER LAKES TRAIL (New York)

The Finger Lakes Trail System is a network of trails in New York with a 557-mile main trunk-line trail that runs from Allegany State Park in southwestern New York to the Catskill Forest Preserve in eastern New York. An additional 400 miles of side trails loop and spur around the main trunk line. The trail system passes through a mosaic of state parks, forests, and wildlife management areas, as well as the Finger Lakes National Forest and more than 400 parcels of private land, sometimes on trails and sometimes on roads. Elevations range from 430 feet near Ithaca, New York, to 2,660 feet in the Catskills. Approximately 380 miles of the Finger Lakes Trail is contiguous with the North Country Trail.

JOHN MUIR TRAIL (California)

The Appalachian and Pacific Crest Trails share a parallel history, so it's no surprise that the Long Trail, Vermont's iconic precursor to the Appalachian Trail, has a western equivalent, the famed 211-mile John Muir Trail, which is contiguous with the Pacific Crest Trail for about 160 miles through the High Sierra.

The notable difference between the John Muir Trail and the Pacific Crest Trail is that the PCT does not go to either the southern or northern terminus of the JMT. The PCT thus misses two of the most iconic spots not only in the Sierra, but in all of the American outdoors: the summit of 14,494-foot Mount Whitney, which is the highest peak in the contiguous United States, and Yosemite Valley, a landscape so famously photographed by Ansel Adams that to enter it for the first time feels—to an outdoorsperson—like coming home. Indeed, the same could be said for all of the John Muir Trail. Ansel Adams's 1938 photographic book of scenes along the JMT was in part what persuaded Congress to set aside lands for Sequoia and Kings Canyon National Park.

The only downside to the John Muir Trail is that it is exceedingly popular. Permits can be hard to get and campsites are crowded—not only with hikers, but also with marauding black bears that have learned the joys of backpacking food. (Bear-proof canisters are required on this trail.) Even so, the allure to wilderness lovers is compelling: the eight high passes over 10,000 feet include some of the most spectacular scenery in the world.

LONE STAR TRAIL (Texas)

Texas's only long-distance hiking trail is the 129-mile Lone Star Trail, a national recreation trail that crosses the Sam Houston National Forest (along with some private parcels of land). Much of the trail is flat (the southern section follows an old railroad bed) with occasional wet sections and bridged creek crossings. Notwithstanding muddy feet, this is a trail where potable water sources are few and far between, requiring hikers to do careful water planning or, perhaps, caching. The Big Creek Scenic Area is a nice highlight, with springtime flowers and (unusual for this trail) plentiful water.

LONG PATH (New Jersey and New York)

The Long Path winds and twists 326 miles from the west bank of the George Washington Bridge in Fort Lee, New Jersey, just north of New York City, to Thacher State Park near Albany. Connecting many of the Hudson Valley's state and public lands, the trail's scenic highlights include the 400-foot-tall Palisades and the climbing mecca of the Shawangunks. In the southern fifth of the trail, however, hikers share these experiences with parkways, traffic, and densely settled communities. The traffic and population density thin as one travels north and enters the Catskills.

OPPOSITE: Lucifer Falls, Finger Lakes Trail, Robert H. Treman State Park, New York

FOLLOWING SPREAD: Timberline Lake, John Muir Trail, Sequoia National Park, California (left); a pack train along the John Muir Trail crossing the San Joaquin River, Kings Canyon National Park, California (top right); Mount Huxley, Evolution Basin, Kings Canyon National Park, California (middle right); the John Muir Trail, California (bottom right)

Trail managers are working on plans to extend the trail into the Adirondacks and connect it with the Northville-Lake Placid Trail.

LONG TRAIL (Vermont)

The Appalachian Trail may be the thousand-pound gorilla with the noisy press agent, but Vermont's Long Trail is the elder statesman, secure in the fact that, born in 1910, it is a good 10 years older than the big, brash upstart—even if that upstart copied its blazes and commandeered part of its route.

The idea for a long trail running down the spine of Vermont is credited to James P. Taylor, who conceived of the idea while sitting atop Stratton Mountain. In 1910, he assembled 23 people into the newly formed Green Mountain Club, which viewed the Green Mountains as a recreational resource and the Long Trail as a way to access them. The new club set about trail clearing on Camel's Hump and Mount Mansfield, and by the time Earl Shaffer's proposal for an Appalachian Trail first saw the light of day, the club had built more than 200 miles of trail, including a system of trail shelters for overnight use. When the idea of the Appalachian Trail took hold, the Green Mountain Club became involved in the project, and the southernmost 100 miles of the Long Trail were incorporated into the Appalachian Trail.

The 272-mile Long Trail is a much more difficult hike than one might think looking at its mostly tree-covered mountains, which have neither the height nor the rugged first impression of the grand mountains of the West. Nonetheless, the northern part of the Long Trail has some of the most difficult hiking to be found anywhere, with steep grades and rock scrambles that are at times comparable to the famously difficult treadway in the White Mountains or the Mahoosucs of New Hampshire and Maine. Don't expect the Green Mountain Club to relocate the trail to easier terrain anytime soon: they like it this way!

MID STATE TRAIL (Pennsylvania)

Pennsylvania is one of the "hikingest" states in the nation: it is the only state to offer three national scenic trials (the Appalachian, North Country, and Potomac Heritage), plus the nascent Great Eastern Trail. The Mid State Trail, called the "wildest trail in the state," is a 523-kilometer network. (The Mid State Trail is one of the few trails in the United States using metric measures: the guidebook explains that,

"Metrication is a patriotic measure designed to help end our cultural isolation." If, however, you think in miles, it's 325 of them.)

The main trunk line, which is mostly complete, runs from the New York State border near Lawrenceville, Pennsylvania, to the Pennsylvania-Maryland border near Flintstone, Maryland. It will also be included in the Great Eastern Trail. Consistent with the demographics of Pennsylvania—densely settled, but with large stretches of rural farmlands and forests—the Mid State Trail has a feeling that is at once both wild and accessible. The backcountry feel of a rocky narrow ridge is often coupled with the convenience of having that ridge be less than a mile from a road.

MOUNTAINS-TO-SEA TRAIL (North Carolina)

The Mountains-to-Sea Trail claims the highest point of any long-distance trail in the East: the summit of 6,684-foot Mount Mitchell, the highest peak east of the Mississippi River. And it goes all the way down to sea level at the Outer Banks. On its western end, it terminates at Clingmans Dome in Great Smoky Mountains National Park, where it connects to the Appalachian Trail. The goal of the Mountains-to-Sea Trail is to be a backbone that connects as many regional trail systems and scenic areas as possible. When finished, the trail will be about 900 miles long; about half is currently completed.

NORTHVILLE-LAKE PLACID TRAIL (New York)

The 133-mile Northville-Lake Placid Trail passes through what many consider the wildest and most remote parts of the Adirondack Park. Dating from 1922, when it was laid out by the Adirondack Mountain Club (ADK), it was one of the club's first projects. The trail is mostly a lowland route, with a high point of 3,008 feet—well below the summits of the surrounding mountains. Perhaps this accounts for its relatively light usage, although the pretty lakeside campsites and shelters certainly offer an outstanding backcountry experience. Lowland north country also means beaver dams (whose presence sometimes necessitates trail relocations, or, at the very least, finding a way around flooded sections of the route) and blackflies (which torment hikers from late spring through the middle of July). The ADK is working on relocations to take the trail off busy highways at or near its ends.

OPPOSITE: The Long Trail between Morse Mountain and Madonna Peak, Mount Mansfield State Forest, Vermont

FOLLOWING SPREAD: Ladders along the forehead of Mount Mansfield, Long Trail, Vermont (left); view north from the Long Trail along Molly Stark Mountain, Vermont (right)

OREGON DESERT TRAIL (Oregon)

Still a work in progress, this 800-mile route runs from its western terminus in the Oregon Badlands Wilderness to its eastern terminus at Lake Owyhee State Park. Crossing mountains, vast deserts, rivers, and canyons, the route is a combination of existing hiking trails, old jeep tracks, and historical wagon roads, with some sections requiring navigation and cross-country skills. Some sections are accessible by foot, horseback, mountain bike, or raft.

OUACHITA TRAIL (Arkansas and Oklahoma)

The 223-mile Ouachita Trail is a national recreation trail that runs through the Ouachita Mountains, mostly in central and western Arkansas, with 46 miles in eastern Oklahoma. Most of the route is within the Ouachita National Forest, with some sections on private land, and two segments in wilderness areas. While the trail's primary use is by hikers and backpackers, two-thirds of it is open to mountain biking. On most of the trail, however, use is light. Elevations range from 370 to 2,610 feet at Rich Mountain on the Arkansas-Oklahoma border. The best seasons to hike are spring, winter, and fall; summer is too hot and too dry for comfort.

OZARK HIGHLANDS TRAIL (Arkansas)

The 218-mile Ozark Highlands Trail in northwest Arkansas can be considered a sister trail to the Ozark Trail. The terrain is similar, with much of the route through the Ozark National Forest. Highlights include White Rock Mountain, Spirits Creek, Hare Mountain, Marinoni Scenic Area, Eldridge Hollow Waterfall Area, and the Hurricane Creek Wilderness Area.

OZARK TRAIL (Missouri)

Primarily a hiking and backpacking trail (but in some places open to biking and equestrian use), the Ozark Trail will eventually reach from St. Louis, Missouri, to Arkansas, where hikers will be able to connect with the Ozark Highlands Trail. Nearly 400 miles of the Ozark Trail are complete, with the eventual length estimated to be about 500 miles. The terrain includes low mountains and knobs, valleys and hollows, bluffs and caves, as well as a diverse array of vegetation and wildlife.

PINHOTI TRAIL (Alabama and Georgia)

The 225-mile Pinhoti Trail starts atop Flagg Mountain in Alabama, the southernmost Appalachian peak with an elevation of more than 1,000 feet. It continues northwest through Alabama and Georgia, where it cuts into Georgia and meets the Benton MacKaye Trail. The terrain is rolling southern mountains that may occasionally rear up with steeper climbs and rockier crags than at first meets the eye—followed by earned views of the mountains of the Talladega National Forest. "Pinhoti" is a Native American word meaning "turkey home," a name that is still appropriate. The Pinhoti Trail is a part of both the Eastern Continental Trail and the Great Eastern Trail.

SHELTOWEE TRACE TRAIL (Kentucky and Tennessee)

The approximately 300-mile-long Sheltowee Trace Trail, a national recreation trail, is named after Daniel Boone, who was given the name Sheltowee, meaning "Big Turtle," when he was adopted by the Shawnee. The trail passes through a region famous in American history, where Boone led hunters on the Wilderness Road and across the Cumberland Gap. In addition to the Daniel Boone National Forest, the trail passes through the Big South Fork National Recreation Area, Cumberland Falls State Resort Park, and Natural Bridge State Resort Park. Almost all of the trail's mileage is in Kentucky, with the remaining few miles in Tennessee. The trail is open to hikers, and in some places open to equestrians and mountain bikers as well.

SUPERIOR HIKING TRAIL (Minnesota)

The Superior Hiking Trail is a 220-mile nonmotorized footpath that follows the rocky ridgeline above Lake Superior in northeastern Minnesota. With trailheads and parking lots every five to 10 miles, the trail is ideal for day hikers and section hikers. It is a designated national recreation trail and is also a proposed segment of the North Country Trail. *Backpacker Magazine* named it one of the 10 best trails in the United States.

As it follows the North Shore of Lake Superior, it climbs over ridgetops, and then descends into creek valleys. Habitats include birch, aspen, pine, fir, and cedar forests, open grasslands and rocky outcroppings, creeks and waterfalls, deep gorges and towering cliffs, and waterfalls and rapids.

TAHOE RIM TRAIL (California and Nevada)

Combining granite Sierra peaks and nearly constant views of the incomparably blue, mountain-fringed Lake Tahoe, the outrageously scenic Tahoe Rim Trail

OPPOSITE: Falls along St. Louis River, Superior Hiking Trail, Jay Cooke State Park, Minnesota

FOLLOWING SPREAD: The Superior Hiking Trail ascending Wolf Rock, Minnesota (left); the Superior Hiking Trail through a birch forest, Minnesota (right)

is a 165-mile loop around the lake on the California-Nevada border. North of the Echo Lakes trailhead just northwest of Tahoe City, about 50 miles of the trail overlap with the Pacific Crest Trail. The Tahoe Rim Trail passes through six counties, one state park, three national forests, and three wilderness areas. The trail is a single-track multiuse path intended for hiking and horseback riding, along with mountain biking, which is permitted except in wilderness areas, Lake Tahoe Nevada State Park, and on segments contiguous with the Pacific Crest Trail.

TUSCARORA TRAIL
(Virginia, West Virginia, Maryland, and Pennsylvania)

The 250-mile Tuscarora Trail was developed in the 1960s as an alternative to the Appalachian Trail and as a response to increasing development along the AT corridor. Today, this blue-blazed alternate route forms a loop with the Appalachian Trail, joining it near Carlisle, Pennsylvania, and Front Royal, Virginia. In between, it passes through forests of oak, hickory, pine, and mountain laurel along the mountain ridges and valleys of Virginia, West Virginia, Maryland, and Pennsylvania. This trail eventually will become part of the Great Eastern Trail, which will extend from Alabama to western New York. Note that the southern part of the trail in Virginia is sometimes referred to as the "Big Blue," after the color of its blazes.

WILD CARDS

Nature doesn't often follow straight lines, and trails don't always fit neatly into categories. The four trails below are much shorter than the other trails in this book, but are included because they each offer something completely unique.

CHILKOOT TRAIL (Alaska)

Running smack across the US-Canadian border, the Chilkoot Trail is a historic 33-mile route originally used by 19th-century prospectors moving from Dyea (near Skagway, on Alaska's southeast coast) to Bennett, British Columbia, in Canada, and from there to the Yukon gold fields of the 1890s. The trail is in the Klondike Gold Rush International Historical Park, managed jointly by the United States and Canada. Only 50 backpackers are allowed on the trail each day.

Rising from sea level in the coastal rain forest, the trail climbs to 3,500 feet at Chilkoot Pass—a brutal, treeless, snow-covered elevation at a high latitude. Backpackers have it easy compared to the so-called stampeders (the name given to the miners who first crossed the pass). Before stampeders were permitted to cross the pass, the Canadian government required them to have a year's worth of supplies to survive on the frontier; the list of required essentials added up to two tons per man. Most of the men ferried their possessions, going up and down the pass as many as 80 times to carry more and more loads weighing 50 to 60 pounds each up and over. And, like modern hikers starting a thru-hike with too much of the wrong stuff, they sometimes abandoned nonessentials. Today, the cold air of the alpine pass has preserved some of these artifacts, giving the Chilkoot Trail the claim of being the world's longest outdoor history museum.

Today's hikers generally take three to five days to complete the hike, traveling south to north (the direction in which the prospectors traveled) and passing through three distinct ecosystems: the coastal rain forest, the high alpine section, and the boreal forest. The hiking season extends from late May through early September.

KALALAU TRAIL (Kauai, Hawaii)

It's a mere 11 miles, although out and back makes it 22, and you have no choice about that: there's no other way out once you go in. But Kauai's famed Kalalau Trail on the rugged, unusual Napali Coast is truly unique. The Napali Coast comprises a series of "palis"—in Hawaiian, "fingers"—of steep, mountainous coastline that plummets into the ocean. Once used by native Hawaiians to grow taro, the land here is rugged, steep, and, today, inaccessible to anyone but hikers. There are no roads, and no other paths: just this single precipitous hiking trail that hugs the cliffs, climbing from sea level to 800 feet and then back down again, passing hanging valleys, side trails to waterfalls, caves, and beaches (where strong currents can make swimming dangerous). Views of the mountain-framed ocean line up one better than the last, with an alternating palette of lush green vegetation against purple and red rocks speckled with wildflowers and birds. The trail winds its way around, down, and over five valleys before reaching its end at Kalalau Beach, where the sheer cliffs prevent any further hiking.

The trail can be hiked one way in a day, but most hikers enjoy breaking it up and taking a bit more time. Long shadeless stretches in the heat of midday can

contribute to heat exhaustion. The first two miles of the trail are popular with day hikers, who climb for a mile, then descend to Hanakapiai Beach before turning around and retracing their steps.

LOST COAST TRAIL (California)

This 25-mile trail makes the list because it is one of only a handful of wilderness coastal hiking experiences in the contiguous United States. This mostly flat walk hugs the exact place where land meets sea at the base of the rocks where the King Range plunges into the Pacific Ocean. Initially slated to be developed as part of the Pacific Coast Highway, the wilderness was saved when engineers got a firsthand look at the cliffs and the ocean and skedaddled inland to build the road in a more sane location.

It's not even fully passable for hikers: ocean waves can be dangerously high and pound in over the trail, spring snowmelt can swell streams that run down from the mountains, and some parts of the route are passable only at low tide, so carry tide tables and bring your patience. Indeed, taking your time is good advice for the whole trail: figure at least three days to enjoy the sea lions, sea otters, tidal pools, and wildflowers. This hike through Bureau of Land Management lands can be crowded in summer; spring and fall offer more chances for solitude.

WONDERLAND TRAIL (Washington)

Washington's Wonderland Trail is the nation's premier loop trail, a 93-mile circuit around Mount Rainier. It is an extremely challenging hike, with some 22,000 feet of elevation gain spread over its length. Most hikers take 10 to 14 days to complete the circuit, the mileage to some extent determined by camping permits, which are required by Mount Rainier National Park, and which are available by lottery in the spring.

Hikers are almost always climbing or descending as they circumambulate the trail and pass through its various ecosystems, from coniferous forests to

OPPOSITE: The Lost Coast Trail near Sea Lion Gulch, King Range National Conservation Area, California

RIGHT: A rock cairn along the Lost Coast Trail, King Range National Conservation Area, California (top); a southern section of the Lost Coast Trail along Chemise Mountain, King Range National Conservation Area, California (bottom)

subalpine meadows to the trail high point of 6,750 feet, well above the tree line at Panhandle Gap. Throughout, Mount Rainier rises overhead, looming, glaciated, impressive. The best time to hike the trail is late summer, when the snows have melted, the bugs have subsided, and the winter storms have yet to start rolling in.

MEGATRAILS IN THE MAKING

It takes decades to build a trail of 1,000 miles or more. Most long-distance trails start with an intention: usually, to showcase a certain kind of environment or geological feature, or to link together existing trails to create longer routes.

At first, ultralong trails may simply be collections of preexisting trails that already go through many of the nation's premier wildernesses and backcountry areas. Road walks and cross-country travel link the sections until permission is received to cut and mark connecting trails. Recognition by land-management agencies must be granted for trails to be blazed and to appear on government maps. Slowly, people start to hike on these new routes. Constituencies are built supporting not only the trails, but also the preservation of the lands through which they pass. Conflicts may arise: between user groups, between users and land managers, between land managers and planners, lawyers, developers, local politicians, or private landowners. In the meantime, hikers keep coming, walking on trails where possible, roads where necessary. Web journals are published, sharing routing information. Advocates keep advocating. "It's like water dripping on rock," said Ron Strickland, whose decades-long effort to create the Pacific Northwest Trail followed this pattern. "I just keep dripping." And slowly, a new trail is born.

The routes described below are all in the midst of some part of this process. Not every new megaroute that has been proposed is included, and those that have not yet established firm supporting trail organizations or government recognition have been omitted.

Long-distance trail networks can be many things: they can represent the dreams of their founders, they can connect small communities to the people who cherish the wildlands surrounding them, they can be playgrounds, challenges, and churches—or they can be little more than collections that link together preexisting trails for the benefit of the record books or for a few ultrastrong hikers who will become momentarily

famous for hiking longer, faster, or through worse weather than anyone else.

But for every long-distance hiker who makes the papers striking a triumphant pose on a mountaintop or beside an ocean, there are tens of thousands of others who simply like to walk in the woods. And on a long trail, what all hikers have in common is a sense of the possibilities—whether it's the dream of the next ridge or of a horizon a thousand miles away. Those dreams are what created, and what continue to fuel, the long-distance trail system. Here, in order of increasing length, are some of the longest walking routes in the United States.

CALIFORNIA COASTAL TRAIL (California)
This 1,200-mile route is a discontinuous path from Oregon to Mexico. It consists of a braid of different and approximately parallel trails intended to meet the needs of different kinds of users, from cyclists to hikers to equestrians to beach walkers. The trail also detours around sensitive environmental sites, including nesting areas. The goal is for the trails in the system to always be within sight, sound, or at least scent of the sea.

GREAT EASTERN TRAIL (Alabama to New York)
Linking together a series of already existing and in-progress "shorter" long-distance trails—including the Allegheny, Tuscarora, Mid State, Cumberland, and Pinhoti Trails, among others—the Great Eastern Trail is intended to provide a 1,600-mile hiking experience in the western Appalachian Mountains. It will offer a quieter alternative to the increasingly popular Appalachian Trail from Alabama to New York. About 70 percent of the trail's route currently exists as a series of interlinked preexisting trails.

GREAT WESTERN TRAIL (Mexico to Canada)
The Great Western Trail is another network of routes that hopes to resolve the conflicts that sometimes arise with multiple uses on trails by developing a braided network of interconnected, related trails, allowing for noncompeting mountain biking, hiking, equestrian, and motorized uses. The current routing includes 4,455 miles of trail from the Mexican to Canadian borders through Arizona, Utah, Idaho, Wyoming, and Montana. Passing through environments ranging from deserts and canyons to plateaus and woodlands to alpine tundra, it showcases the ecology and geology of the western states.

OPPOSITE: The Florida Trail heading toward the Great Eastern Trail, Blackwater River State Forest

The Great Western Trail was designated Utah's Centennial Trail in 1996 as part of the celebration of Utah statehood; it became a National Millennium Trail in 2000; and it is currently being considered for inclusion in the National Trails System.

EASTERN CONTINENTAL TRAIL
(Florida to Newfoundland and Labrador)
The so-called Eastern Continental Trail (estimated length: 5,400 miles) has no official status, but it comprises a series of recognized components and has become visible enough in the long-distance community that it deserves inclusion here.

Starting in Key West, the route follows the paved Florida Keys Overseas Heritage Trail to the mainland where it joins the Florida Trail near the Everglades. The route follows the Florida Trail to the Alabama border. Starting on Alabama back roads, the route returns to hiking footway on the Pinhoti and Benton MacKaye Trails. At Springer Mountain, the route jumps on the Appalachian Trail for its entire journey to Katahdin in Maine. From there, it follows the International Appalachian Trail first to Cape Gaspé, Quebec (the original terminus), and then to Belle Isle (the Newfoundland and Labrador island that is the current terminus). If you're up for it, figure a year of your life.

AMERICAN DISCOVERY TRAIL
(Delaware to California)
This 6,800-mile-long route from Delmarva Peninsula on the Atlantic Ocean to Point Reyes on the California coast is championed by the American Hiking Society. The trail cuts through the heartland of the United States, and includes a northern and southern loop in its midsection. A handful of hardier long-distance hikers have tackled the whole thing; some have done it as a combination hiking-biking trip.

SEA-TO-SEA ROUTE (Quebec to Washington State)
Much of the routing necessary to hike from Cape Gaspé at the Atlantic Ocean in Canada to the Olympic Peninsula on Washington's Pacific coast is either already in place or in progress: a hiker can start at Cape Gaspé, walk down to the Appalachian Trail to Vermont, cut north on the Long Trail to arrive near the North Country Trail, and then follow the NCT west to North Dakota. In North Dakota hikers would need to follow a series of country roads all the way to Glacier National Park in Montana, but once there, they can pick up the Pacific Northwest Trail and coast a mere 1,200 miles to the Pacific.

INTERNATIONAL APPALACHIAN TRAIL
(Maine to Newfoundland and Labrador . . . and Beyond?)
The International Appalachian Trail began as the proposal of Richard Anderson, a Maine marine biologist who remarked that the Appalachians didn't stop atop Katahdin, so why should the trail? The observation spawned an international effort, beginning at the northern terminus of the Appalachian Trail atop Katahdin and continuing north to the Canadian border. From there, the new International Appalachian Trail went to Cape Gaspé at the edge of Quebec. And that, at first, was the end of it.

Mountains. Sea. Stop.

But long-distance hikers, it turns out, aren't thwarted by a mere obstacle like the North Atlantic Ocean. Only a ferry ride separates Cape Gaspé from Labrador and Newfoundland, where another 800 miles of mountains related to the Appalachians beckon. The International Appalachian Trail was extended and became 1,900 miles long, nearly as long as the AT from Georgia to Maine.

You'd think *that* would be the end of it. But once again, science stuck its head into the mix: geologists theorize that the Appalachian Mountains and the mountains of Western Europe and North Africa are kissing cousins, both of them relics of a 250-million-year-old chain of Central Pangean Mountains that existed on the giant supercontinent Pangaea. When Pangaea broke up, its mountains split into new- and old-world segments.

Long-distance hiking visionaries being what they are, eyes looked to new horizons. In April 2010, a Greenland chapter joined the International Appalachian Trail organization. Scotland joined next, adding its iconic West Highland Way. In 2010, nine new chapters—Norway, Sweden, Denmark, the Netherlands, England, Ireland, Wales, the Faroe Islands, and Iceland—became part of the proposed route, and plans are afoot, in the most literal sense, to add Germany, Belgium, France, Spain, Portugal, and Morocco. The proposed journey makes the original Appalachian Trail truly look like little more than a walk in the woods.

And once again one has come full circle: to the Appalachian Trail . . . and to the power of dreams. The possibilities, and the trails, are endless.

OPPOSITE: Atlas Mountains, Morocco, a proposed route of the International Appalachian Trail

AFTERWORD BY BART SMITH

If America's national parks are indeed the country's best idea—as Ken Burns and Dayton Duncan suggested in their PBS documentary—then its National Trails System is, by extension, a pretty darn good idea as well. I am fortunate to have had time, health, and a supportive family, which allowed me the opportunity, over a period of 18 years, to walk all 11 national scenic trails. I did so carrying an SLR camera, several lenses, and a tripod on top of a backpack already stuffed with camping gear, clothing, and food. The extra 17 pounds of photography equipment burdened my legs and shoulders, but ultimately it lifted my spirits, providing me the tools through which to share my sense of wonder and hopefully convey an appreciation for the remarkable natural heritage along the national scenic trails.

Of course, I didn't originally set out with the lofty dream of walking and photographing the more than 18,000 miles of America's National Scenic Trails System. That would be crazy. But I did start the Pacific Crest Trail on July 28, 1992, with an 80-pound backpack full of camera and camping gear and the lofty dream of walking and photographing the entirety of *that* remarkable trail and ultimately creating a coffee-table book. With refinements to my gear and added muscle on my legs, I was able to lug a 55-pound backpack along the windswept crests of the Sierras, Cascades, and the four other mountain ranges traversed by the PCT. I spent a good part of the next six years alternating between construction work and re-hiking the PCT, always adding new images to my collection. Of all the national scenic trails, it is my humble opinion that the Pacific Crest Trail traverses the widest array of environments and geologic regions. From Anza-Borrego to the Columbia River Gorge, from the Belknap lava flow to Evolution Basin, from Mount Whitney to Mount Rainier, the PCT is a constant exploration through diverging environments. Eventually I did contribute my images to a coffee-table book covering the Pacific Crest Trail (written by Karen Berger) and I felt I was on a path to following my bliss.

If I was to keep this bliss thing going, however, I needed another trail. Being a Washingtonian and well versed with the steep slopes of the Cascade Mountains, I figured that walking the Appalachian Trail would be, well, a walk in the woods, and I would have new environments to explore along the "granddaddy of all trails." A few days into my AT journey, however, another nickname for the trail became evident: the "green tunnel." Gone were the halcyon days on the PCT, the endless views in all directions. On the AT, it is common to walk up, up, and up to a sign in the woods designating the top of the mountain, and then down, down, and down. Hauling all that metal and glass up and down the green tunnel, through the humidity and lightning storms of the East Coast summer, was testing my newfound bliss. But I learned to be receptive to the foreign environment and once again my photographic muse was challenged and rewarded with intimate landscapes along the forest floor—Dwarf iris, Pink Lady's Slipper, even periodic vistas of receding ridges of the ancient mountains. I essentially hiked the trail over a two-year period, selecting long sections I thought might best display a certain season: North Carolina and Tennessee in spring, New Hampshire and Maine in autumn, Maryland in winter, and so forth.

With the bliss thing generally working out, I spent a better part of the next decade hopping from one national scenic trail to the next. If I had to pick an absolute favorite section along the entire National Scenic Trails System, it would be the Florida Trail through the Big Cypress National Preserve. The trail is often submerged through the cypress swamp and, if it has been raining, just finding a campsite can be disheartening. But I have never felt such a profound feeling of transcendence into the wilderness as those first 60 miles from the southern terminus of the Florida Trail. Another environment I found beguiling was the sphagnum bogs along the Ice Age Trail. They are meadows of grasses and tamarack floating on top of kettle lakes in the final stage of entropy. The North Country Trail is arguably the most ambitious, over-the-top trail in the system, which is to say it was right in my wheelhouse. It is so long—more than 4,000 miles—that only 12 intrepid souls have walked its entirety. But "the dirty dozen" is all-inclusive and more than willing to expand its fraternity of wanderers and welcome others to experience the Great Lakes region the old-fashioned way: one step at a time.

By the time I found myself running from yet another lightning storm along the Continental Divide Trail, I thought it was going to be my last national scenic trail. Not because the bliss thing was losing its luster (though it was severely tested), but rather because completing the CDT in 2008 meant that I had walked and photographed the entire National Scenic Trails System. Until 2009, that is. For almost 30 years, the National Scenic Trails System comprised eight trails. With the passage of the 2009 Omnibus Public Land Management Act, three new trails were added to the system. So on I walked along the Arizona Trail through the great Sonoran Desert, along the New England Trail over traprock buttresses, and finally along the Pacific Northwest Trail, ending with a sunset over the Pacific Ocean.

To say I don't have a favorite trail may sound lame, but I sweated buckets, cursed now and then, experienced mystery, experienced awe, and felt profound gratitude on all 11 national scenic trails.

THE NATIONAL TRAILS SYSTEM: A WORK OF CITIZEN STEWARDSHIP

America's 11 national scenic trails (and 19 national historic trails) exist through the work of a small group of federal trail managers, professional staff of several nonprofit trail organizations, and thousands of citizen volunteers. Throughout the National Trails System those volunteers contribute more than one million hours annually to build new trails and maintain existing trails and the natural and cultural resources along them. This citizen stewardship of national public resources is a very special characteristic of the National Trails System that distinguishes it from all other national resource preservation systems.

This essential involvement of citizen stewards in nearly all aspects of the national scenic trails stems from Benton MacKaye's 1921 proposal for a trail along the length of the Appalachian Mountains and a tradition of citizen trail making in New England and the Appalachian region. MacKaye did not suggest that the newly formed National Park Service or the United States Forest Service should create the long-distance trail. Rather he called for citizens from the smoggy cities to come to the healthy, clean air of the mountains during their vacations to build the trail by working together in community camps. He foresaw great physical and mental health benefits for the people engaged in trail making, as well as benefits of sociability in the communities of interest that the project would foster.

The formation of the Appalachian Trail Conference in 1925 provided a framework for organizing and guiding the experiment to create the long-distance trail through a network of shared responsibility along its projected route. This approach was emulated in the 1940s, '50s, and '60s by organizations formed to create the Pacific Crest, Ice Age, and Florida Trails.

In 1968, when Congress established the National Trails System, it respected and honored the culture of citizen stewardship that was flourishing along the long-distance trails. Rather than creating a National Trails Service as a sister agency to the Park Service and Forest Service to develop and sustain national scenic trails, it recognized the essential roles that volunteers had played in creating the Appalachian Trail by authorizing and directing the federal agencies to involve citizens and their nonprofit organizations in virtually all aspects of managing these trails. This was as conservative and radical an action by Congress as Benton MacKaye's proposal to create a 2,000-mile-long Appalachian Trail through the work of citizens was 47 years earlier.

Now, 46 years after the creation of the National Trails System, all 11 national scenic trails remain works in progress. There are more than 3,000 miles of gaps in the continuous off-road paths these scenic trails are intended to be, requiring sometimes long road walks for hikers seeking to walk the "entire" trail. Through our collective federation, the Partnership for the National Trails System (PNTS), the citizen organizations sustaining these trails are working to greatly increase the public and private funding and other resources needed to close many of these gaps by the 50th anniversary of the National Trails System in 2018.

Enjoy the adventures these long-distance pathways make possible and the varied landscapes through which they pass while remembering that they are works in progress. Please help us complete and sustain these national resources by becoming a member of one or more of the organizations supporting them, by contributing to any of these organizations or PNTS, and by joining the volunteers in maintaining existing trails and building new trails. Experience the joy and satisfaction of being a steward of America's premier hiking trails.

GARY WERNER
Executive Director, Partnership for the National Trails System
www.pnts.org

SUGGESTED READING LIST

Along the Arizona Trail
Jerry Sieve

Along the Florida Trail
Sandra Friend, photographed by Bart Smith

Along the Pacific Crest Trail
Karen Berger and Daniel R. Smith,
photographed by Bart Smith

Along Wisconsin's Ice Age Trail
Eric Sherman and Andrew Hanson III (editors),
photographed by Bart Smith

"An Appalachian Trail: A Project in Regional
Planning," *Journal of the American Institute
of Architects*
Benton MacKaye

*The Appalachian Trail: Calling Me Back
to the Hills*
Earl Shaffer, photographed by Bart Smith

*The Appalachian Trail: Celebrating
America's Hiking Trail*
Brian King and the Appalachian Trail
Conservancy

The Appalachian Trail Reader
David Emblidge (editor)

*A Blistered Kind of Love: One Couple's
Trial by Trail*
Angela and Duffy Ballard

Desert Solitaire
Edward Abbey

The End of Nature
Bill McKibben

Faith in a Seed
Henry David Thoreau

The Florida Trail Guide
Sandra Friend and John Keatley

Guide to the Natchez Trace Parkway
F. Lynne Bachleda

*Hiking the Triple Crown: How to Hike America's
Longest Trails*
Karen Berger

*I Promise Not to Suffer: A Fool for Love Hikes
the Pacific Crest Trail*
Gail Storey

The Journals of Lewis and Clark
Meriwether Lewis and William Clark

*Long-Distance Hiking: Lessons from the
Appalachian Trail*
Roland Mueser

My First Summer in the Sierra
John Muir

*The North Country Trail: The Best Walks,
Hikes, and Backpacking Trips on America's
Longest National Scenic Trail*
Ron Strickland

Of Men and Mountains
William O. Douglas

On the Beaten Path: An Appalachian Pilgrimage
Robert Alden Rubin

On the Trail of the Ice Age
Henry S. Reuss

The Pacific Crest Trail: A Hiker's Companion
Karen Berger and Daniel R. Smith

Pacific Crest Trail: Northern California
Jeffrey P. Schaffer

Pacific Crest Trail: Oregon and Washington
Jeffrey P. Schaffer and Andy Selters

Pacific Crest Trail: Southern California
Ben Schifrin, Jeffrey P. Schaffer, Thomas
Winnett, and Ruby Johnson Jenkins

Pacific Northwest Trail Digest
Tim Youngbluth

*The Pacific Northwest Trail Guide: The Official
Guidebook for Long-Distance and Day Hikers*
Ron Strickland

*Pathfinder: Blazing a New Wilderness Trail
in Modern America*
Ron Strickland

*River Pigs and Cayuses: Oral Histories
from the Pacific Northwest*
Ron Strickland

Sierra Nevada: The John Muir Trail
Ansel Adams

Walden
Henry David Thoreau

*A Walk in the Woods: Rediscovering
America on the Appalachian Trail*
Bill Bryson

Walking the Appalachian Trail
Larry Luxenberg

Walking with Spring
Earl Shaffer

Wanderlust: A History of Walking
Rebecca Solnit

*Where the Waters Divide: A Walk along
America's Continental Divide*
Karen Berger and Daniel R. Smith

*Wild: From Lost to Found on the Pacific
Crest Trail*
Cheryl Strayed

TRAIL ORGANIZATIONS

LONG-DISTANCE HIKING

American Long-Distance Hiking Association–West: www.aldhawest.org
Appalachian Long-Distance Hikers Association: www.aldha.org

APPALACHIAN TRAIL

Appalachian Trail Conservancy: www.appalachiantrail.org
National Park Service: www.nps.gov/appa

ARIZONA TRAIL

Arizona Trail Association: www.aztrail.org

CONTINENTAL DIVIDE TRAIL

Continental Divide Trail Coalition: www.continentaldividetrail.org
Continental Divide Trail Society: www.cdtsociety.org

FLORIDA TRAIL

Florida Trail Association: www.floridatrail.org
Florida Trail Hikers Alliance: www.floridatrailhikes.org

ICE AGE TRAIL

Ice Age Trail Alliance: www.iceagetrail.org
National Park Service: www.nps.gov/iatr
Wisconsin Department of Natural Resources: dnr.wi.gov/topic/parks/
name/iceagetrail/

NATCHEZ TRACE TRAIL

National Park Service: www.nps.gov/natt

NEW ENGLAND TRAIL

Appalachian Mountain Club: www.outdoors.org/conservation/trails/
new-england-national-scenic-trail.cfm
Connecticut Forest and Park Association: www.ctwoodlands.org/NET
National Park Service: www.nps.gov/neen
New England Trail: www.newenglandtrail.org

NORTH COUNTRY TRAIL

National Park Service: www.nps.gov/noco
North Country Trail Association: www.northcountrytrail.org

PACIFIC CREST TRAIL

Pacific Crest Trail Association: www.pcta.org

PACIFIC NORTHWEST TRAIL

Pacific Northwest Trail Association: www.pnt.org

POTOMAC TRAIL

National Park Service: www.nps.gov/pohe
Potomac Heritage Trail Association: www.potomactrail.org

First published in the United States of America in 2014
Rizzoli International Publications, Inc. | 300 Park Avenue South | New York, NY 10010 | www.rizzoliusa.com

© 2014 Rizzoli International Publications, Inc. | Text © 2014 Karen Berger | Photography © 2014 Bart Smith | Foreword © 2014 Bill McKibben

Project Editor: Candice Fehrman | Book Design: Susi Oberhelman | Map Illustrations: James Daley and Philip Bibens

The Partnership for the National Trails System (PNTS) connects member nonprofit trail organizations and federal agency partners to further the protection, completion, and stewardship of the 30 national scenic and historic trails within the National Trails System. For more information, visit www.pnts.org/get-involved

For interactive versions of the maps in this book, as well as specific information on any of the national scenic trails, please visit the national trails page on the National Park System website: www.nps.gov/nts/nts_trails.html

The national scenic trail emblems are official federal insignia protected from unauthorized use by the provisions of 18 U.S.C. 701.

2019 2020 2021 2022 / 11 10 9 8

Printed in China | ISBN-13: 978-0-7893-2741-3 | Library of Congress Catalog Control Number: 2014936348

PAGE 1: The Pacific Northwest Trail through Big Beaver Valley, North Cascades National Park, Washington; PAGES 2-3: The Continental Divide Trail toward Front Range, Routt National Forest, Colorado; PAGES 4-5: The Pacific Crest Trail through Grouse Meadows, Kings Canyon National Park, California; PAGE 331: The North Country Trail near Highbanks Rollway, Manistee National Forest, Michigan; PAGE 332-336: A variety of hiking gear; FRONT COVER: Stoney Indian Trail section of the Pacific Northwest Trail, Glacier National Park, Montana; BACK COVER: Old Trace, Natchez Trace Trail, Mississippi

National Scenic Trails System

More than 18,000 miles

- Appalachian Trail (1968)
  Approximately 2,200 miles

- Arizona Trail (2009)
  Approximately 800 miles

- Continental Divide Trail (1978)
  Approximately 3,100 miles

- Florida Trail (1983)
  Approximately 1,400 miles

- Ice Age Trail (1980)
  Approximately 1,200 miles

- Natchez Trace Trail (1983)
  Approximately 444 miles

- New England Trail (2009)
  Approximately 215 miles

- North Country Trail (1980)
  Approximately 4,600 miles

- Pacific Crest Trail (1968)
  Approximately 2,700 miles

- Pacific Northwest Trail (2009)
  Approximately 1,200 miles

- Potomac Heritage Trail (1983)
  Approximately 800 miles

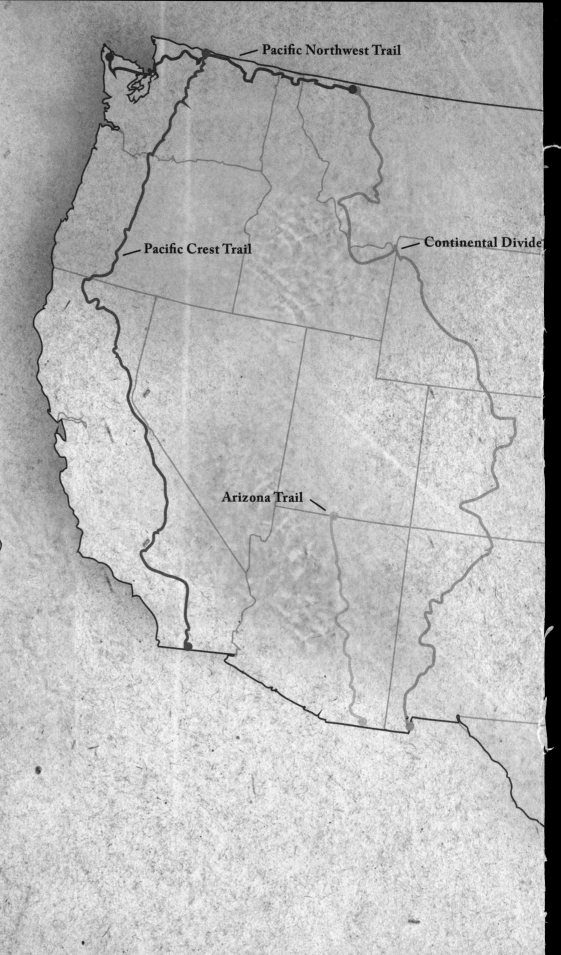

Pacific Northwest Trail

Pacific Crest Trail

Continental Divide

Arizona Trail